VISIBLE STRENGTHS

VISIBLE STRENGTHS

Capitalize on Strengths,
Contribute Value,
and Communicate Results
to Accelerate Your Career

MARY MOSOPE ADEYEMI

NEW DEGREE PRESS

VISIBLE STRENGTHS

Capitalize on Strengths, Contribute Value,
and Communicate Results to Accelerate Your Career

ISBN

979-8-88504-582-7 *Paperback*

979-8-88504-927-6 *Kindle Ebook*

979-8-88504-698-5 *Digital Ebook*

To my father, Chief Fidelis Adesoji Olufemi Adeyemi (of blessed memory).

You are one of the most significant influences in my life. As I sat to write each chapter of this book, the stories and lessons kept leading me back to you.

Thank you for loving me, teaching me, sacrificing for me, listening to me, and modeling everyday leadership. You were a true reformer, and your legacy lives on in me. I wish you were here to see your baby girl fly, but I know you are with me in spirit.

This book is a homage to you. Continue to sleep well.

Contents

INTRODUCTION   9

CHAPTER ONE   MY VISIBLE STRENGTHS   23

PART 1   **CAPITALIZE ON STRENGTHS**   **45**

CHAPTER TWO   DISCOVER YOUR STRENGTHS   47

CHAPTER THREE   DISCOVER MORE STRENGTHS   65

CHAPTER FOUR   CLARIFY WHAT MATTERS   79

CHAPTER FIVE   MANIFEST YOUR VISION   97

CHAPTER SIX   PLAY TO YOUR STRENGTHS   123

SUMMARY: CAPITALIZE ON STRENGTHS   139

PART 2   **CONTRIBUTE VALUE**   **143**

CHAPTER SEVEN   DEFINE VALUE   145

CHAPTER EIGHT   DELIVER VALUE   159

CHAPTER NINE   MIND YOUR MANNERS   183

CHAPTER TEN   DELIVER TOGETHER   203

CHAPTER ELEVEN   OWN YOUR POWER   229

CHAPTER TWELVE   RESPOND TO SELF-DOUBT   249

CHAPTER THIRTEEN   PRIORITIZE YOUR HEALTH   269

SUMMARY: CONTRIBUTE VALUE   289

PART 3   **COMMUNICATE RESULTS**   **293**

CHAPTER FOURTEEN   MARKET YOURSELF   295

CHAPTER FIFTEEN   BE VISIBLY VALUABLE   309

SUMMARY: COMMUNICATE RESULTS   319

CONCLUSION: CONTINUE THE CYCLE   321

ACKNOWLEDGMENTS   329

BIBLIOGRAPHY   337

Introduction

"The beauty of your career is the journey of figuring out what you are uniquely gifted at and how you can use it to add value to others in a brilliant, bright, and sparkly way."
— Mary Mosope Adeyemi

****

Have you ever wondered what it takes to have a fulfilling and successful career? Have you ever wondered how others have achieved this in their careers?

Imagine if you could get all that information without trial and error. This book sets out to help you achieve that.

Before we begin, I would like you to consider three questions about your career:

1. Is your work crafted around your natural gifts and talents?
2. Can you use those talents to solve problems for the people and organizations you serve?

3. Do the relevant people know that you exist and are worthy of their attention and sponsorship?

If you answered *yes* to these questions, consider yourself lucky. If you answered *no*, don't worry. That response is more common than you might think.

If someone had asked me these questions fifteen years ago when I started my career in finance, my answers would undoubtedly have been a combination of *somewhat*, *sort of*, and *unlikely*! Yet, by turning those answers into *yes*, *yes*, and *yes*, I have grown in my career to become an executive director at a leading investment bank—proof of what timely intervention and support can do.

A whole new world opens up when you leave the petri dish of the formal education system. The ten- to twelve-week terms, assignments, open-book exams, self-selected project teams, meritocratic grading systems, and mandatory spring and summer breaks are left behind. The time has come to generate a return for the years of academic investment and create economic pathways.

Everyone faces many decisions about the type, style, quality, pace, and location of the careers they pursue. Some will go for what brings excitement and fulfillment, some will join only innovative or "sexy" industries, some will follow their peers and friends, and others will go for what will bring them the most financial gain. Whatever the case, those decisions need to be made with some intentionality to give oneself a fighting chance at success.

Unfortunately, this is rarely the case. Many begin their careers with little preparation, only to find themselves in one of these scenarios:

1. By a stroke of luck, they land in the perfect spot. They are growing, delivering, and earning. It all worked out.
2. On the surface they are doing well, but they lack fulfillment. They are in a job that affords them the life they want to have. Yet, every day, they can't connect with their why, impact, or how they are growing. They are not happy but are trapped by the feeling that there is no way out.
3. Nothing is working. They have tried and failed at many career options and hit a dead end. Neither their work nor their money is satisfactory.

Whichever scenario you identify with, you always have the opportunity to accelerate, reposition, or fully reset your career. If you are doing well, you can do better. If you are not doing as well as you would like, you can get back on the right track.

A LITTLE BIT ABOUT MY CAREER PATH

I started my career in 2006 at the age of nineteen with great ambition and motivation to excel. Early on, I identified that the most straightforward pathway was to get excellent grades in school and secure good work experience. So, while studying for my undergraduate degree in Accounting and Finance at Lancaster University, I secured a summer internship at Deutsche Bank and began my first foray into banking.

A couple of years later, after completing my master's in management at Imperial College Business School, I accepted a full-time role as a credit analyst in the London office of Bank of America (BoA) right in the middle of the 2008 global financial crisis. I came in with bright eyes and a bushy tail, ready and excited to start my ascent up the proverbial career ladder.

Unfortunately, it didn't take long before that excitement wore off. I slowly realized that my technical competence and "work hard" strategy were not fully translating into the perception others had of me at work. Surrounded by high-achieving type-A professionals, I was not standing out. Although I was doing good work, I repeatedly received feedback that I was "not visible" but couldn't understand why.

Especially as a Black woman working in a predominantly white and male industry, I was convinced I was hyper-visible by default. *So why couldn't they see me?*

After unsuccessfully doing everything to be seen, I inevitably internalized this feedback as code for: *we don't see you because you are Black or not like us.* Eventually, I believed that people like me could not be successful in these types of organizations.

Years later, with strengths coaching and the support of a key sponsor, I learned the pivotal lesson that the visibility I sought was not just about being physically seen. Instead, that visibility was about using my strengths to add value and then communicating this value to others.

Getting this support and gaining this awareness when I did was game changing. I was happier, more energized, and more productive when I started operating in my strength zone. When I started focusing on adding value, I built my credibility and people cared more about me. When I began sharing my results, many more opportunities came my way.

My career success accelerated because I made my strengths visible.

THE EVIDENCE

Still, I reflect on my career with awe and wonder how that confused young girl stayed on the path and grew into a seasoned professional. Like many, I used to think that a career was something that happened to you rather than something you created on purpose. Thankfully I know better now, but I often wonder how many professionals do not.

This curiosity and interest led me to spend thousands of hours developing, executing, and managing talent recruitment and training and development programs along with working in my functional role as a risk manager.

My experience then ignited a burning passion that became viSHEbility, a social-first organization I founded in 2018 whose mandate is to improve outcomes for professionals in the marketplace through inspiration, coaching, community, and advocacy.

Through my work, I have had the privilege of speaking with, recruiting, managing, mentoring, and coaching thousands of professionals, especially *early careers*.

In this book, early careers include those in the first five years in the workplace, those transitioning to new career fields, and those stepping up into an elevated role. By age, these individuals will fall into the millennial (born between 1981–1996) and Gen-Z (1997–2012) generations, which are signaling significant dissatisfaction in the workplace.

This group of individuals repeatedly asks questions such as: How do I discover my strengths? How can I gain more confidence? How can I grow my network? How can I be more visible in my workplace? How can I be paid more?

In 2019, I surveyed three hundred early career professionals across diverse sectors to determine their top career challenges. Their responses were consistent and instructive, and their struggles are organized into four categories here:

1. **Clarity**: they lack clarity on what path to take toward and through their career
2. **Confidence**: they lack the confidence to articulate their strengths or present their work in a way that attracts new opportunities
3. **Community**: they lack the sticky and sustainable relationships necessary for progression in the workplace
4. **Coaching**: they lack access to personal development programs that prepare them for the workplace and equip them with strategies to succeed

THE VISIBLE STRENGTHS PHILOSOPHY

You'll get no shortage of advice on finding fulfillment and success in your career. Every time I have spoken with high-achieving people, their responses have varied as widely as their experiences and present priorities. They say: Find your passion, do only work that you love, try new things, exceed expectations, network, find a sponsor, be visible, and much more.

As helpful as their advice is, it can also be overwhelming and may not be applicable or transferable across industries, jobs, and experience tiers. This got me pondering: What "through-line" career advice can professionals apply in all circumstances?

What I found has transformed the way I see the future of career success. To find fulfillment and success in your career, you should apply what I have coined as the **Visible Strengths Philosophy**.

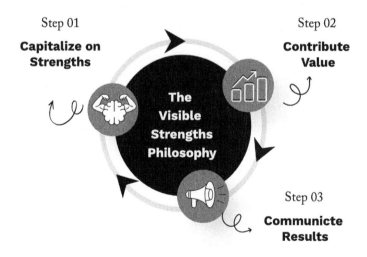

1. **Capitalize on strengths**: Leverage your strengths in everything you do. They are your most significant area of opportunity because you start with what comes most naturally to you. Unfortunately, according to Gallup, only four in ten people at work believe they are in jobs where they get to do what they do best daily.

2. **Contribute value**: Solve problems and you will always be in demand. You must understand what is considered valuable to those you serve and deliver those relevant results consistently and innovatively. No one can argue with value.

3. **Communicate results**: Work doesn't speak; people do. You need to master the art of telling others the story of the work you are doing or have done, how you have done it, and why it is the solution to their most pressing problems. Communicating results is the key to being recognized and adequately compensated for your work. You cannot empower, influence, or rise to significance if you are not visible.

If you can cut through the echo chamber of the career and business advice you have received, you will realize that at any stage of your career, in any industry, and in any seat you occupy, it all boils down to these three elements: strengths, value, and visible results.

I have leveraged this three-step process to execute transactions and projects and foster new business and personal relationships. Then, I realized that it was repeatable, transferable, and most importantly, scalable to a broader philosophy. This process is more than a tool. The Visible Strengths Philosophy is a mindset you should adopt for how to execute your career.

As our pace of life accelerates and the modern world of work evolves, an increase in the demand for a portfolio career is expected. "More than half (52 percent) of Gen-Z are expecting to have multiple careers during their working life, with 43 percent viewing a portfolio career with several jobs or employers as a desirable way to live." (Henley Business School, 2019)

Portfolio careers offer the opportunity for people to operate across diverse industries, geographies, and contract types because they seek to acquire new skills, explore new options, enjoy new experiences, and open up multiple streams of income.

Consequently, adopting the Visible Strengths Philosophy will empower you to break through all mental limitations you may have placed on what you can do or where you could work. You would become more agile and better respond to the ever-changing work landscape. You would be free to move between departments and organizations, roles and professions, countries and continents, because the formula remains the same. Whether you apply it to achieve such success is up to you.

WHO IS THIS BOOK FOR?

Over the years, I have taught the Visible Strengths philosophy. I have seen it positively impact professionals working at some of the most prestigious companies in the world, such as McKinsey & Company, Accenture, J.P. Morgan, Goldman Sachs, Bank of America, Lazard, IFC, and Barclays, among many others.

I have hosted and listened to hundreds of interviews and conversations with some of the most seasoned career and business professionals and read mountains of career books and articles. The insights I have gained and my personal experiences contribute to over 10,000 expert hours that form the basis of this book.

I have written *Visible Strengths* for you, the determined and ambitious early career professional who does not want to follow the trial-and-error approach in their career. This book is for you who want to build your credibility quickly in the workplace while remaining authentic to yourselves. I wrote it for you who want to use every opportunity to shape your careers by telling the story of who you are and how you serve; for you who want a diverse and exciting career that grows you, provides for you, and inspires you to continue reaching higher heights; for you who want an excellent career, not a mediocre one.

I have also written *Visible Strengths* for you, the seasoned professional who wants to accelerate, reposition, or fully reset your career. Let this book remind you how you can continue to show up powerfully.

I welcome career coaches and counselors to leverage this book for mentoring, teaching, and coaching. Take from it or add to it; just know that I am grateful you are an advocate of *Visible Strengths*.

I also encourage employers and managers to use this book to coach and guide your junior and mid-level employees who embody the highest risk of leaving organizations. According to Deloitte's Global 2022 Gen Z and Millennial Survey, "Four in ten Gen Zs and nearly a quarter of millennials would like to leave their jobs within two years, and roughly a third would do so without another job lined up." With an overemphasis on executive coaching, the opportunity for early-career intervention for the junior talent pool is often missed. If you invested in them only a fraction of the time and money you do for your executives, you would build a bench of self-aware, engaged, productive, confident, and valuable talent motivated to help your organization achieve its goals. You would also save yourself and your company tremendous chaos and cost due to turnover and hiring replacements.

Finally, entrepreneurs can apply this book's philosophy and principles. You can learn to use your strengths in your business to visibly add value and attract new customers, suppliers, advocates, sponsors, and much more.

I hope that at the end of this book, you will receive three things: clarity on your path, confidence in your choices, and the courage to define your success and step into what you want to achieve.

WAIT, BEFORE YOU JUMP IN: THE VISIBLE STRENGTHS VIRTUAL HUB

As a thirty-five-year-old woman writing this book in 2022, I recognize that while I have some nuggets to share today, I still have much life to live and much to learn. The thoughts and advice in this book will be impactful and transformational, but I am open to how these may evolve.

I may want to add to my findings or change my mind on some things. Who knows?

I have created the Visible Strengths Virtual Hub to leave room for this growth. This space will host many resources to deepen your learning on the topics explored in each chapter, including:

- Worksheets for each chapter
- Book and podcast recommendations
- Blog posts and articles
- Interview clips
- Events
- Signposts to other helpful content and much more

The goal of the virtual hub is to create a living evergreen book that honors your growth and mine. As psychotherapist and author Diane Barth said, "The point of success is not about achieving a one-time goal. . . . Instead, it is a feeling of accomplishment that should propel you to continue the process."

My success with this book is that you learn enough to recognize that the journey doesn't end here. Instead, your journey is only beginning! When you stick with it through the ups and downs, you will realize that the beauty of your career is the journey of figuring out what you are uniquely gifted at and how you can use it to add value to others in a brilliant, bright, and sparkly way.

So, what are we waiting for? Let's capitalize on your strengths, contribute value, and communicate your results.

CHAPTER ONE

My Visible Strengths

"Start where you are. Use what you have. Do what you can."
—*Arthur Ashe*

****

Have you heard the phrase, "Use what you have"?

This statement means different things to different people and is often used to let someone know they already have something within reach which can be used to solve a problem.

"Use what you have" is one of my favorite statements because it is an instruction with a promise. It instructs us to look within and around ourselves for the necessary tools. It also holds a powerful promise that if we only learn to identify and apply these tools, we are already well on our way to fixing what is broken around us.

Similarly, *Visible Strengths* is an instruction with a promise, instructing you to identify your strengths and make them visible through the value you create. That instruction holds the promise that when you do this, you will unwrap the career of your dreams.

At least, that has been my experience.

HOME LIFE

I was born in June 1987 in Lagos State, Nigeria to a middle-class family.

My father, Chief Fidelis Adesoji Olufemi Adeyemi, was an accomplished man. With an undergraduate degree in Business Administration, a postgraduate degree in Public Administration, and a range of executive programs in public finance and development studies, my father valued academic proficiency in himself and others.

After a brief stint in the private sector as a consultant, my father moved to public service in 1970 as a junior administrative officer. Although my father stayed loyal to the public service, he built a dynamic and multifaceted career spanning twenty-four years. He worked with the Ministry of Education; the Ministry of Commerce and Industry; the Civil Service Commission; the Deputy Governor's office; the Ministry of Local Government and Chieftaincy Affairs; the Ministry of Health; the Ministry of Establishments, Training, and Pensions; the Plans, Programmes, and Budget Bureau; and the Ministry of Finance and Economic Development. He served at various times and in numerous capacities, learning on the job, gaining experience, and adding immense value.

In recognition of his track record of exceptional delivery, he was appointed as Secretary to the Lagos State Government and Head of Service in 1994, hitting the summit of the public service.

In 1996, his administration was retired from public service, which gave him the time and space to refocus on his passion for continuing education. He founded GREIDAMS (Gregorio Institute of Development, Administration, and Management Studies). Here, he wrote and delivered 149 papers and 162 workshops to thousands of middle and senior management executives from the Lagos State Government.

My mother, Chief (Mrs.) Elizabeth Omotayo Adeyemi, was also in public service as a health worker. In her twenty-six-year career, she studied, worked, and led health practice in child and maternal care, disease control, and nursing. She retired as Chief Nursing Officer and joined my father to run the training practice, serving as the Director of Human Resources and Catering.

My parents were not born with a proverbial silver spoon, but with much grit they achieved enough to ensure that I was born with one. They were the first to teach me that a little can amount to much if you lead with value and generosity.

ON THE MOVE

After a quality primary and secondary school education in Nigeria, I moved to the United Kingdom in 2004 at sixteen years old. Sending their kids abroad in hopes of better tertiary academic opportunities was not unusual for Nigerian parents who could afford the exorbitant international school fees.

"Remember who you are and where you are coming from," my parents would say. This was both a threat and an encouragement to follow the path and example of excellence they had set for me. Their advice is the North Star that still guides me in everything I do.

My mum would repeat a cautionary tale of a friend's son who was sent abroad for higher education but mixed up with the wrong crowd. He got into trouble and was detained by the authorities for months without bail. Consequently, he failed to complete his education and could only get menial labor jobs. After about five years, he returned home with "nothing to show for it." I would never know whether this was a real story or a scare tactic. Either way, it drove home the message.

After completing a nine-month foundation course, I was admitted to Lancaster University in 2004 to study for a Bachelor of Arts in Accounting and Finance. These were two of my best subjects in school. I had a natural affinity for them, so I didn't resist when my father suggested a degree and future career in accounting. He had such a profound influence on my academics and career choices, teaching me to explore my interests and seek out opportunities proactively.

For me, university was about exploring fields of study that I found interesting. Alongside my majors, I signed up for electives in Economics, Statistics, Law, and Operations Management. If it sounded interesting, I signed up until I maxed out the permitted number of units. Though hectic, the learning experience was enjoyable.

While in the second year of my three-year degree, I started applying for internship programs. Although it was my preference then, I was unsuccessful with my applications to accounting firms. Still, I got my foot in the investment banking door with support from Sponsors for Educational Opportunity (SEO) London. This charity helps ethnic minority professionals access careers across many sectors.

Providence had brought SEO my way when they participated in a career fair at my university. I could not attend the talk that day because it clashed with a lecture, but a friend of mine did and shared their flyer with me. Unbeknownst to her, that flyer would change my life.

You see, my university, while good, was not one of the prestigious Oxbridge or Russell Group universities where employers rushed to set up recruitment stalls. So having SEO London come to my campus to talk about their work and recruit for leading banks based in London was akin to a once-in-a-lifetime event. I submitted my application to the SEO program on December 22, 2005. I got the call to attend the assessment center a few weeks later.

I had little to no idea what an investment bank did or what job opportunities were available within the industry. I even recall being on the train from Lancaster to London for the assessment center day when I searched "what does an investment bank do?" on Google. I knew it was a long shot, but I did not let that stop me.

My parents were an example of unlikely success, yet they made it work by trying. They motivated me to focus on what I had—good technical knowledge from my courses, the gift of the gab, and my ambition—rather than what I lacked. These qualities seemed to do the trick, and I secured one of the coveted investment banking placements.

After weeks of pre-training organized by SEO, I started my career on the Global Banking desk at Deutsche Bank in 2006. That summer was hard, but I learned a lot about myself and what I might like to do. I got to learn about banking and the varied opportunities it provided. I didn't love the desk I was on, but I felt for the first time that banking, rather than accounting, was the way to go.

After the summer, I went back to Lancaster to complete my degree. I graduated with a First Class and returned to the "street" for another summer placement in 2007, this time on the Portfolio Management desk at BoA. I loved this desk because it intersected with my love for analytical work and client delivery. It paid well and had relatively reasonable hours. Thankfully, I secured a full-time job to start after I completed my master's in management at Imperial College. I started my full-time job in 2008 at BoA. As a credit analyst, my job was to assess prospective credit investments and provide a recommendation to my senior approvers. This job was perfect for me!

I often wonder if I would have been able to secure an internship if SEO did not support people like me. I am grateful to them for giving me the jump start I needed. SEO and many other catalyst organizations still exist today, helping individuals from underserved communities to access their chosen careers. With a simple Google search, you can find a few online. Many organizations have created in-house programs to attract a diverse talent pool. These are a lifeline for many professionals like they were for me.

FAILURE TO LAUNCH

Now in the workplace and surrounded by type-A—that is, driven, competitive, and aggressive—personalities, I was one of many fish in a small pond with limited space, food, and resources. I had been around brilliant people before, but typically in those cases, there was a mix of abilities. This was my first time in a more competitive and less diverse environment, and I was intimidated and scared.

Like everyone else, I was working hard. Still, I observed that I was being passed over for high-value assignments that were pivotal for my learning and career progression.

During feedback meetings with my managers, I would get statements like these:

"Mary, you are technically strong, but I don't think people know that."

"Mary, you know your clients, but your clients don't know you."

"Mary, you need to be more visible."

I am not a petite or quiet person by any stretch of the imagination. As I've stated before, as a Black woman working in a predominantly white and male industry, I was convinced that I was hyper-visible by default. I felt I stuck out like a sore thumb and could not understand what my managers meant by "be visible." I was physically present, so why couldn't they see me?

In response, I started doing everything to be seen. I planned work events, took on more work than everyone else, joined affinity groups, and participated in recruitment activities. I was everywhere but nowhere at the same time. Eventually, I internalized my managers' feedback as code for: *We don't see you because you are Black or not like us.*

The implications of my invisibility also felt more acute with the backdrop of the 2008 global financial crisis. Additionally, in 2009, my firm made a transformational acquisition of Merrill Lynch. For about five years, the company and its employees experienced so much change. I went through eight managers in the first four years of my career. I had to be adaptive as the emerging company underwent restructuring while navigating a difficult season for the industry. The company's size grew, the core function of my department evolved significantly, and so did our alignment in the corporate structure.

At that time, many colleagues lost their jobs due to role redundancy, so naturally I also lived in constant fear of being fired. I felt that if I drew too much attention to myself or fell short just by a little bit, I would be on my way out of a job.

These feelings of inadequacy are prevalent among those who consider themselves a minority in the workplace. This could be on the basis of gender, race, socioeconomics, sexuality, or ability. Often, minorities feel they are the last to be hired but the first to be fired when the opportunity arises. The burden of the minority also rests on these employees' shoulders, meaning they bear the fear (and in some cases, the reality) that one person's mistakes are inadvertently translated to members of the same group. This causes them to shrink back at work rather than show up with boldness.

THE LIGHTBULB MOMENT

Four years into my career in 2012, something changed. I got a new manager, Ade, a peculiar and intelligent individual who, in hindsight, was my first career sponsor. He had been in another department at the firm for many years and moved to lead our team. He was also Nigerian, so I was inspired by the fact that he was a director and he represented something that I had not yet seen.

Until then, I had been the only Black person on my floor of more than one hundred people. I had not seen people more senior than me that were Black or of African heritage. Subconsciously, this reinforced my cultivated belief that Black people like me could not be successful in my department or the firm. Ade joining my department burst that limiting belief, and that singular point was encouraging.

Beyond that, Ade took a keen interest in me. I was the only associate in my team at the time, supporting many vice presidents in executing transactions and portfolio monitoring work while training the analysts in the group. For context of where I ranked, in banking, you would typically go from Analyst, to Senior Analyst, to Associate, to Vice President, to Director, and then to Managing Director.

In one of our earliest meetings, Ade asked me to outline my responsibilities.

"What do you do for the department or firm beyond your immediate team?" he asked.

I paused.

"Not much at the moment," I responded. "But in the past, I have helped with recruitment events."

I didn't think I was doing anything noteworthy at the time, so I deviated. I took the opportunity to share that improving my visibility was a key area of focus and had been cited as the reason I was being overlooked.

"More people need to know who I am," I explained.

"Why?" he responded.

"Well . . . they need to know my name and the work that I am doing."

"Why?" he asked again. "Why should they care about who you are and the work you do?"

I stared at him, still unclear about where he was going with this line of questioning.

"Who are those you impact with your work? For instance, your key stakeholders. What are the department's goals for this year? What high-value clients are you looking after?"

He then explained, "People would only care about you or the work that you are doing if it is relevant to their goals. If it doesn't make a difference to them, it doesn't matter. You need to articulate how your work is valuable to the team, the department, and the firm right now."

The penny started dropping.

He was teaching me the pivotal lesson that this visibility I sought was not just about being physically seen. Instead, it was about adding value and seeking ways to communicate those relevant results to those they matter to.

This conversation has been one of the most eye-opening and influential in my career. I had been focusing on the wrong thing and failed to learn how to create stories around my work.

THE FOCUS ON STRENGTHS

Gaining this awareness was only the first step in the journey. Ade could see that I had lost myself after years of receiving nonconstructive feedback. I needed to reconnect with what I did well before plugging the gaps. He referred me for training programs focused on rebuilding confidence, relationship building, and influencing. The most insightful were the coaching sessions on strengths. In the program, I worked on a few exercises that helped me become more aware of my natural talents and learned strengths.

Of these exercises, the most impactful was the CliftonStrengths (then known as Clifton StrengthsFinder) assessment that highlighted my top five signature strengths, which were:

- Responsibility: my sense of responsibility, ownership, and commitment
- Relator: my ability to foster close relationships with others to achieve a common goal
- Learner: my passion for learning and continuous improvement
- Significance: my desire to do meaningful work and be known for the work that I do
- Restorative: my ability to figure out and resolve problems

Before this, I had an inkling of what I was good at from my observations, such as my strong analytical skills, meticulousness, being a hard worker, and ability to think critically. I had seen these manifest at school and work. However, I had not done the deep work needed to discover more of my natural talents, learn how to communicate them to others, or understand how I would make them work for me in the workplace.

For example, I can now articulate that responsibility helps me take on and complete challenging tasks. Relator helps me bring the right people together to deliver a project. Learner helps me understand my clients and industries better. Restorative helps me troubleshoot problems and provide solutions for the firm and our clients. Significance—that is, seeing and feeling the impact of my work on a company, my clients, and those around me—is important to me. I need to do purposeful work that makes a difference in people's lives.

A better knowledge of my natural talents and acquiring the language I needed to articulate them changed how I approached my work. For the first time, I could see that I embodied the knowledge, skills, and attributes to succeed in my credit analyst role. I just needed to lean into them more.

With this awareness, I was challenged and encouraged to seek opportunities to use my strengths daily and add tangible value.

VISIBLE STRENGTHS IN PRACTICE

The pathway to success was more evident than I thought. If visibility relied on creating value and value relied on being aware of and utilizing my strengths, then that created a repeatable cycle: the Visible Strengths philosophy.

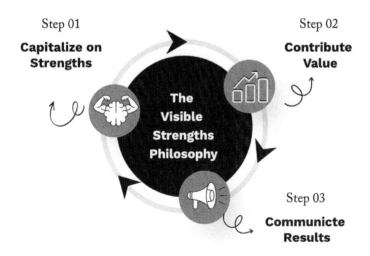

1. **Capitalize on strengths:** I need to leverage my strengths in everything I do.
2. **Contribute value:** I need to solve problems so I will always be in demand.
3. **Communicate results:** I need to tell the story of the work that I am doing or have done.

Completing the cycle led to opportunities to capitalize on my strengths, contribute more value, and communicate more results. Fortunately, an opportunity to test the elements of the Visible Strengths Philosophy presented itself soon after its conception.

A client, a leading global supplier of foreign currency exchange, approached the firm with a high-value mandate. Our bank was supposed to supply physical bank bills to support its institutional wholesale business on an ongoing basis. This mandate meant an attractive piece of business, and many senior leaders were excited about the prospects. This was the first time executing such a product for any client in Europe. We had no blueprint to follow, which created the opportunity to be innovative.

With Ade's support, I joined the transaction team as the lead credit manager even though I was only a senior associate. This assignment was part of a pack of changes that Ade made to ensure a more balanced allocation of high-value clients that had historically been reserved for a select few colleagues. Although I was initially intimidated, I knew this was a unique opportunity to learn and show what I was made of.

This is how I leveraged my Visible Strengths to succeed in this project.

I CAPITALIZED ON MY STRENGTHS

I considered my role on the transaction team and all the things I had in my toolkit that would give me an advantage:

- In the past two years, I had attended meetings with the client's group treasurer and had fostered a close working relationship with him, so they were open to my ideas and advice.
- I had good knowledge of the client's services, customers, and financial performance.
- As the credit representative on the transaction team, I was familiar with our bank's New Product Review (NPR) approval process. I had previously supported a few NPR approvals and had a history of working with the committee members, which gave me the insight I needed to guide the team through the process.
- My analytical, detail-oriented, and organized core skills made me an effective business analyst and project manager. The fact that I was an associate was an advantage because I spent more time on the details relative to my senior business partners.
- My law studies at university and experience negotiating commercial agreements were very helpful when dealing with the client's representatives and ensuring that the bank was in the best position possible by the end of the process.

Regardless of how busy the days were, each day on that transaction left me energized because I was leveraging my strengths. I knew my work mattered, and I was uniquely talented to support its execution.

I CONTRIBUTED VALUE

I understood that success for the client meant delivering the requested bank bills by a specific date, and success for the bank was completing all internal and external investigations and approval processes to ensure that the firm took no unnecessary risk. Any action that moved us closer to delivering those was relevant and, consequently, valuable.

In order to tangibly outline the value I contributed, I boiled my contributions down to a list of completed deliverables:

- I participated in multiple meetings with my colleagues and the client, ensuring that I gathered all the information needed for the NPR.
- I went on an operational site visit to the vault to understand what physical controls were in place to protect the bank.
- I negotiated the bank bill facility agreement alongside the lawyers.
- I wrote the required sections of the NPR approval memo and advised the other strands of the deal team on how to complete theirs.
- I presented the credit risk thesis to the approval committee and addressed their concerns.

Although it took six months, all this led to successful transaction approval. Our deal team also won an internal award for "The Most Innovative Product" that year and delivered millions of dollars for the firm. Our business development teams developed a blueprint and gained more confidence in marketing this product to other clients.

I COMMUNICATED MY RESULTS

This is where I struggled most.

I have always been a hard worker. Growing up, my parents would tell me, "fi akitiyan sinu iṣẹ rẹ, yoo san," which is Yoruba for "Work hard and it will pay off." This is good advice, but it takes more than just working hard.

Ade impressed upon me the importance of not just doing good work but making sure that I let people know, see, and benefit from the work that I was doing. He taught me that work doesn't speak; people do. He encouraged me to share my work, what I was learning, and the results we were generating.

Using biweekly emails, I kept the project leads up to date with our team's progress. I shared:

- A summary of findings from our internal and external discussions
- Any surprises that came up along the way as we engaged with external vendors like the security and insurance companies

- Our plans for the next two weeks and requests for support from senior management
- Any noteworthy updates to the project timeline

I'm not going to lie: these emails were tedious and seemed like overkill. After doing all the "real" work, I spent hours crafting and wordsmithing these update emails till I was blue in the face.

I detested writing them until I recognized the positive impact they were having. I received calls and emails with acknowledgments and follow-up questions, which told me that key people cared about what I was spending time on. The broader committee of stakeholders began to pay attention to who I was because of my contribution and impact.

I was invited to critical closed-door meetings and asked to advise other global teams on this new product I had helped get approved and executed. Eventually, I created a process template for the product and wrote a policy manual so that the department had a consistent approach to this.

The more valuable I showed myself to be, the more critical and influential my voice became. Finally, I understood what Ade was trying to tell me about the importance of value-led visibility.

Twelve months later, I achieved my promotion to vice president. Many of the MDs on the project team served as references and sponsors for my promotion. The comments in my review now read, "Mary is a highly regarded credit professional with a good track record of being able to influence and negotiate outcomes whilst maintaining effective client and stakeholder relationships." A complete one-eighty!

Getting support and gaining self-awareness when I did was game-changing. When I started operating in my strength zone, I was happier, more energized, and more productive. When I started focusing on adding value and sharing my results, people cared more about me and gave me opportunities to do more.

My career success accelerated because I made my strengths visible.

SCALING MY VISIBLE STRENGTHS

After this experience, I continued to apply these three elements to new projects. Before long, I realized they were transferable and, more importantly, scalable.

When it comes down to it, careers are a sum of projects. Each offers a fresh opportunity to capitalize on strengths, contribute value, and communicate results. Progressing in your career is contingent upon how well you make use of the opportunities that present themselves in different ways in your life.

Each time I made changes, I went back to the drawing board to complete a strengths audit and plug gaps, focused on delivering what I established as most important to my stakeholders, and carried out the vital work of sharing my results. I had learned that if I focused on these three things as

I joined new teams, departments, firms, and even industries, they would continue to serve me.

I have adopted this mindset and philosophy in my career, and I encourage you to do the same.

YOUR TURN!

Before we go further, use these exercises to gauge where you are right now.

1. Project: Think about a recent project you worked on. How did you apply the three elements of the Visible Strengths Philosophy?
   - I capitalized on my strengths by:
   - I contributed value by doing:
   - I communicated the following results:

2. Career: Reflect on your current job. How are you applying the three elements of the Visible Strengths Philosophy?
   - I am capitalizing on my strengths by:
   - I am contributing value by doing:
   - I am communicating my results by:

If nothing comes to mind, be assured that this is very common. Answering these questions was initially challenging for me as well.

The chapters that follow will guide you on how to discover your strengths and craft your career around them, help you understand how to be most valuable in any environment, and, finally, teach you some strategies for compelling storytelling and visibility.

At the end of this book, we will return to these exercises and celebrate the transformation that I am certain you will experience.

PART 1

CAPITALIZE
ON STRENGTHS

Leverage your strengths in everything that you do.

Your strengths are your most significant area of opportunity because you start with what comes most naturally to you.

CHAPTER TWO

Discover Your Strengths

(FROM WITHIN)

*"Learn what makes you excellent, starting
with your strengths."*

—*Gallup*

****

How much time have you spent thinking about your strengths lately?

In my experience, many people have a vague idea of their strengths but fail to do the deep work to discover them. Instead, we are often taught to fixate on our weaknesses.

My parents constantly challenged me to strive to be excellent and not just good enough. Especially in school, passing was not enough; I had to be number one. One year in secondary school, I recall coming home with the third highest grade in my class. Ordinarily, high grades would be considered an outstanding result received with excitement, but my parents met my grades with both enthusiasm and scrutiny. They congratulated me on the As, and then analyzed how I did not achieve the top score in other subjects.

The following academic year, I studied harder on those subjects, often to the detriment of others. I spent fewer study hours on the subjects I naturally excelled at and did not perform as well in the exams.

As time went on, this parental pressure reduced, but it had become so ingrained in me to overcompensate in areas of development.

This pattern of behavior followed me into university and the workplace. When I had feedback meetings with my managers, I would leave those meetings with only the highlighted areas of development ringing in my ears.

It did not matter to me that colleagues and bosses viewed me as having strong analytical abilities, execution capabilities, commercial awareness, and being a keen developer of people. All I was fixated on were my areas of development, which were usually around tailoring my communication style to my audience, expanding my network, and increasing my visibility.

In response, I took courses on those topics, joined practice groups, and attended numerous networking events to improve in those areas. Don't get me wrong: seeking to improve oneself is always helpful. However, magnifying my weaknesses so much that I didn't leave mental room to acknowledge and appreciate my strengths was a negative approach to growth.

Upon reflection, you may find that, like me, you are caught in the trap of emphasizing your weaknesses over your strengths. You are not alone in this, and it's more common than you think. This behavior is what psychologists refer to as negativity bias, a human tendency to overlook good things and pay more attention to the bad things that happen, making them seem much more important than they are (Cherry, 2020).

In the workplace, this negativity bias forces you to over-invest in trying to overcome your weaknesses while under-investing in your strengths when, in fact, you should be "spending roughly 80 percent of your time on making strengths stronger, and 20 percent improving specific weaknesses that are holding you back from being brilliant at your job" (Tupper and Ellis, 2019). It also keeps you frozen in a space where you focus on what may be "wrong" about you, which is not a positive headspace.

On the other hand, Gallup, a global analytics and advice firm and the administrators of the CliftonStrengths assessment, found that people who are focused on using their strengths in the workplace are six times more effective and engaged in their role, observe an 8–18 percent increase in performance, and are three times more likely to report having an excellent quality of life than those that don't.

They also found that these people are more energized, rested, happy, and confident, and are less worried, stressed, angry, or anxious. Overall, they are more likely to achieve their goals.

If you lack clarity on your strengths or don't have the appropriate language to communicate them to others, it's not too late to fix that. I was five years into my career before I started doing the necessary work to discover my strengths. This chapter will guide you on how to define and discover your strengths beginning from within.

WHAT ARE STRENGTHS?

When I ask people how they define strengths, I often get these responses: what I am good at, what I am trained to do, what I like to do, what I do better than others, or what comes naturally to me.

Another definition struck me from a rather unlikely source. I was watching an episode of *Dragon's Den*, a British reality TV show. Deborah Meaden, one of the Dragons, asked the pitching team of Cheese Geek a question: "So, guys, where is your value? What's the really hard thing to replicate?"

I found this to be a profound way of indirectly defining strengths. Whether you are a digital marketer or software designer, you are hired to do your job because you bring to the table a unique combination of tools that is hard to replicate. These together are your strengths.

Gallup also offers a formula to define strengths, show below:

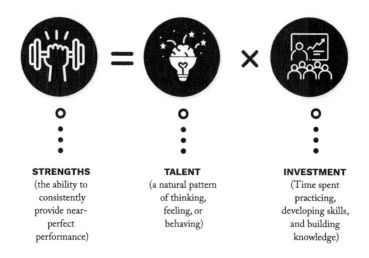

STRENGTHS
(the ability to
consistently
provide near-
perfect
performance)

TALENT
(a natural pattern
of thinking,
feeling, or
behaving)

INVESTMENT
(Time spent
practicing,
developing skills,
and building
knowledge)

I love this formula because it does two things. It places in our hands the power to turn our natural talents into active strengths by investing in them (i.e., by practicing using them and adding knowledge and skill to them). It also highlights the responsibility that we have to put in the work. If you do not invest in your talents, you will not cultivate them into strengths.

Take Kemi, for example. She was born with a natural talent for drawing. As a child, her abstract drawings were more advanced than her peers and evoked strong emotions from those who viewed them. She had something special. At college, she studied art and design, learned techniques, and practiced drawing in different environments. After graduation, she secured a job as a junior designer at the Fashion House.

A few years later, Kemi enrolled in specialized 3D drawing and Computer-Aided Design (CAD) courses. Upon completion, Kemi recognized that she could use these advanced skills in various industries, including animation, manufacturing, shoe making, and many more.

She successfully switched jobs six months later to an architectural design firm where she designs beautiful technical drawings using computer software. Although Kemi had a natural talent, if she had not invested in it through study and practice, it would not have developed into a strength on which she could make a living.

DISCOVER YOUR STRENGTHS FROM WITHIN

Grab a pen and a sheet of paper and set a timer for three minutes.

In this time, write down ten to fifteen things you consider to be your strengths. Don't limit yourself to those that you use at work. Think broadly and include your hobbies and activities with your family, friends, and community groups. They all contribute to your package of strengths.

How many were you able to write down in the allocated time?

If you found that exercise challenging, you are in good company. Often, we find it uncomfortable to think about what we are good at because we believe it makes us seem arrogant, but it doesn't. Turning talents into strengths is an accomplishment worthy of your acknowledgment and pride.

If you're struggling to come up with strengths, reference the **KASHI framework** shown below with five categories to help you explore your strengths.

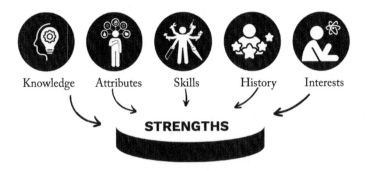

Knowledge Attributes Skills History Interests

STRENGTHS

KNOWLEDGE

This is the theoretical and practical understanding of a subject matter that contributes to your thought leadership. This comes from your academic and professional studies, research, interaction with an issue, and work experiences. For example, your knowledge of coding languages, financial reporting, and common and statutory law would fit into this category.

ATTRIBUTES

These are the qualities or characteristics inherent in you, both your natural behaviors—such as intelligence, sense of humor, and kindness—and your learned behaviors—such as resilience, optimism, agility, and adaptability. Attributes can also include observable physical characteristics such as race, gender, and physical ability.

Case in Point: Knowledge and Attributes

Dr. Damilola Fajuyigbe, PhD, also known as Dammy, is the former Head of Scientific and Medical Direction for sub-Saharan Africa at L'Oreal. She started building her knowledge of the sciences very early, studying mathematics, biology, and chemistry. She then completed her undergraduate degree in Medical Biochemistry and acquired a PhD in Molecular Biology.

When I asked her why she decided to take on a grueling four-year PhD research program, she responded, "I am a very curious person . . . I like asking many questions about the same thing repeatedly until I find the right answer. It is not boring to try to solve a problem that no one else has looked at before."

Dammy specifically researched the impact of skin color on photobiological responses. "For many years, what we knew about the effect of the sun was done on white skin. I wanted to create a bigger picture of sun exposure consequences for the whole spectrum of skin colors. I asked, 'How do Black people respond to the sun?'"

Dammy is a Black African woman, so this area of research impacted her directly, which she acknowledged made her work more pleasurable. "It is generally assumed that [Black people] are quite resistant to the sun because we have a low incidence of skin cancer. But in fact, we have other things that we should be concerned about that are caused by the sun. I wanted to look into that to create a full story and go on to see if there are prevention strategies we can put in place." Although it is not a prerequisite, Dammy's physical attribute as a Black woman was a strength that added to her understanding of and affinity for the issues she was researching.

During her studies, she realized that while she loved science, she preferred to work in strategy rather than in the lab. So, after her PhD, Dammy found the perfect role as Scientific and Medical Strategy Manager at L'Oréal. "My role allows me to touch science but also work to create impact by increasing the visibility of dermatologists in Africa." This perfect role was possible for Dammy because of her experience as a scientist and a researcher in the dermatology field.

Dammy's knowledge of biochemistry and dermatology, her natural curiosity, and her physical traits, among other things, equipped her to execute her research successfully and secure the best job. She played to her strengths, and it paid off.

As you consider your knowledge and attributes, ask yourself:

- What do I know? Think about all the subjects you have studied. Is your knowledge bank up to date, or does it need to be refreshed?
- How do I describe myself? You must include the attributes you genuinely embody today rather than the qualities you aspire to have.

Below is a list of qualities to help you identify your own attributes. You may also find psychometric assessments helpful for giving you the language you need to describe yourself. We will discuss this further in Chapter Three.

Achiever	Adaptable	Bold
Agility	Aggressive	Balanced
Ambitious	Accuracy	Capable
Accountable	Adventurous	Committed

Confident	Imaginative	Patient
Connected	Hospitable	Persistent
Courageous	Ingenuity	Positive
Collaborative	Insightful	Proactive
Competitive	Intelligent	Resourceful
Consistent	Influential	Results driven
Creative	Inquisitive	Respectful
Cooperative	Integrity	Risk taker
Decisiveness	Independent	Passionate
Diligent	Innovative	Persuasive
Dependable	Inspiring	Pragmatic
Detailed	Knowledgeable	Punctual
Disciplined	Loyal	Reliable
Determined	Logical	Responsible
Diversity	Leader	Self-starter
Efficient	Mature	Stability
Empowered	Mentor	Strategic
Educated	Motivated	Speedy
Enthusiastic	Nurturing	Thoughtful
Experienced	Organized	Thorough
Fair	Optimistic	Team player
Focused	Ownership	Trustworthy
Flexible	Open-minded	Understanding
Growth	Originality	Uniting
Humorous	Objective	Visionary
Honest	Persevering	Wise

SKILLS

These are the abilities you naturally possess or have developed through life or work experiences or structured training. For example, selling, digital skills, presenting, problem solving, collaboration, and leadership would be considered skills.

HISTORY

This is the evidence of successful outcomes from actions taken at home, school, work, or elsewhere. History includes your past life and work experiences and your reputation for achieving results which increase the likelihood of continued success. For example, a background in the military is valuable to a leadership role and supports the probability that you will know how to navigate your role as a leader.

Case in Point: Skills and History

Dr. Ola Brown is the founder of Flying Doctors Healthcare Investment Company (FDHIC), a company that invests in and operates across the African healthcare and wellness value chain.

"The death of my youngest sister in Nigeria at twelve years old made me acutely and painfully aware of the challenges with African healthcare systems," Dr. Brown wrote in an article on Medium. "I became determined to try to be part of the solution."

With this clear motivation in mind, Dr. Brown went to work as a medical doctor. Shortly after medical school, she set up an air ambulance business to address the problem of massive distances between hospitals and poor road infrastructure in West and Central Africa. She didn't know much about logistics, but she understood the situation deeply, and her history as a medical doctor gave her credibility.

Over the years, Dr. Brown transitioned into the medical finance space, which she believes is a more impactful seat than that of a practicing medical doctor. She remains "fascinated by how capital deployed in the right way could become such a transformative catalyst for change, particularly in emerging markets."

To equip her for this journey, she read widely. She undertook a slew of post-graduate executive education programs to build her knowledge of economics, project finance, infrastructure investing, banking, and capital markets. She also took personal development courses to develop her business negotiation and marketing skills.

Her work paid off. As of March 2020, FDHIC has invested in nine companies across nine sub-sectors within the health, wellness, and fintech space with a combined valuation of over two hundred million dollars. In 2021, they announced fundraising for a second fund to deepen their investment capacity in the fintech and healthtech spaces.

Dr. Ola continues leveraging her academic and work history as a medical doctor while growing her capabilities with structured training and work experience in finance. The evidence of her success with the air ambulance business and the investments in the first FDHIC fund provides credibility to her capacity to deliver, reinforcing it as a strength.

Many people discount particular life and work experiences before critically thinking about the value of the transferable skills they have picked up along the way. New mums return to work, dismissing months of maternity leave where they have effectively learned to run the operations of the ship called home.

Career changers are often too quick to disregard their past work history from their CV because they feel it is irrelevant.

As you consider your skills and history, ask yourself:

- What can I do? What do I do naturally? What is easy for me to learn? Write out all the skills you have developed over time.
- What have I done before? Where do I have evidence of success? Include all the jobs you have ever had, including family roles, household chores, and volunteer work. Be specific rather than broad as you write them down.

I challenge you to place value on every experience. Each one is part of your story and arsenal of tools.

INTERESTS

These are subjects that fascinate and excite curiosity in you. You are motivated to learn more and do more in these areas. Your interest could be centered on topical socioeconomic issues or fueled by a specific lived experience. For example, you could be interested in the impact of carbon emissions on our environment or the accessibility of funding for women and Black and other ethnic minority business owners.

Case in Point: Interests

For Rolake Akinkugbe-Filani, Chief Commercial Officer for Mixta Africa, her interest in energy jump-started a successful career.

Her fascination with energy stemmed from a lived experience in her childhood which bloomed while she was studying for her post-graduate degree at the London School of Economics. "I still remember nights in Nigeria, using a candle or a lantern to read because there was no electricity," she says. "But the awakening of my mind around the economic development impact of energy didn't happen until after I began exploring the issue academically at university."

Because of this impact on her home country, Rolake felt a call to be a change-maker in this space. "I resolved that whatever happens, I have to do something with energy and natural resources. I have not studied petroleum engineering or anything similar, but I just knew that I had some foundational knowledge and interest. I started to plug myself into anything that could give me exposure."

This interest is a thread Rolake has woven through her successful, international multi-sector career that spans research, finance, investment banking, consulting, and international development with a focus on energy infrastructure. In her current seat, she is crafting and executing the commercialization and market development strategy for a leading infrastructure and housing developer across six African countries.

As you consider your interests, ask yourself:

- What am I genuinely interested in? What do I dream about? What do I worry about? What am I curious about? What am I excited about? What drives my actions?

FEELING FINE FILTER

An important factor often overlooked when thinking about strengths is your feelings.

Your feelings help you differentiate between your strengths and your special or super strengths. Executive leadership coach May Busch defines special strengths as those that "are at the intersection of what you do well and what you enjoy doing."

Assessing the quality of your strengths by your performance and the positive outcome it generates is logical. However, you should also consider the input required to achieve that outcome. More input for the same result is not a good investment.

As leadership coach and author Marcus Buckingham says, "a strength is an activity that strengthens you [and] a weakness is an activity that weakens you—even if you're good at it."

Using this lens, you should review the activities in your daily work routine and determine if they are strengthening or weakening activities. Ask yourself some crucial questions about what makes you feel FINE.

- **Fulfilled**: Do you feel satisfied and happy when doing or after you have completed this activity?
- **Invested**: Do you feel focused, effective, and in-distractable while doing this activity?
- **Natural**: Is this activity intuitive to you? Do you volunteer for it and look forward to doing it?

- **Energized**: Do you feel a burst of energy during or after you have completed the activity, even if you are physically tired?

For example, I think about how I feel when planning an event. Each time, I execute a great event and receive compliments from attendees and other stakeholders. Still, I am often left physically, mentally, and emotionally exhausted, and it takes me a few weeks to recover.

It would be logical for me to view event planning and execution as a strength because the events always go well (history of success) and I get to put my creative, strategic, organizational, and project management skills to use (attributes and skills). However, when I consider the energy I lose each time, I realize that event planning is not a super strength for me.

This assessment is not a one-time event but rather one that requires constant observation. As Donald O. Clifton, the founder of CliftonStrengths, says, "There is one sure way to identify your greatest potential for strength:

1. Step back and watch yourself for a while
2. Try an activity and see how quickly you pick it up
3. Skip steps in the learning and add twists and kinks you haven't been taught yet
4. See whether you become absorbed in the activity to such an extent that you lose track of time

If none of these has happened after a couple of months, try another activity and watch. Over time your dominant talents will reveal themselves, and you can start to refine them into powerful strengths."

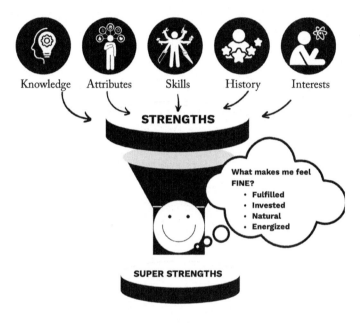

YOUR TURN!

1. Take some time to write at least three strengths under each category of KASHI: Knowledge, Attributes, Skills, History, and Interests. You should find this much easier to do now.

2. Consider the past week or month at work or school. Note the activities that made you feel FINE and those that left you with the opposite feeling.

CHAPTER THREE

Discover More Strengths

(FROM OUTSIDE)

"Feedback is an opinion, grounded in observations and experiences, which allows us to know what impression we make on others."

—*Sheryl Sandberg*

****

Have you ever been given an unexpected compliment? What did you make out of it?

For Sharon, receiving an unexpected compliment was an eye-opening experience. Sharon had been working with her new manager for about six months. During one of their regular coffee chats, her manager said to her, "I don't know how you stay so organized in the middle of all the daily chaos at the office. I appreciate how you help me stay on top of the deliverables."

Sharon was taken aback. She had never considered whether she was organized or not. "It's no big deal," she responded. "I forget things, so I habitually set reminders for everything."

Sharon had failed to identify this as a natural talent and underestimated the value her organizational skills added to her manager.

You may be unknowingly doing the same. Since strengths are formed from natural talents, they are often not objectively observed by us, or we take them for granted because they are simply part of who we are.

Suppose you find that you are the go-to person in your family for advice and information. This could mean that you are empathetic or resourceful. If you are the person that others ask to proofread their CV, job application, or proposal, it could indicate that you pay a lot of attention to detail or have excellent written communication skills.

By leveraging psychometric assessments and external feedback from others, you can enhance your strengths discovery process and uncover talents you didn't know you had.

PSYCHOMETRIC ASSESSMENTS
Psychometric assessments enable talent and personality discovery through scientific tools.

From personality tests to leadership tests, assessment tools to evaluate your strengths are widely available. Some of my favorite tools are:

1. **CliftonStrengths by Gallup**: This assessment measures the presence of talent in thirty-four themes that classify your pattern of thinking, feeling, and behaving that comes naturally to you. These factors drive your ability to think strategically, execute, influence others, and build relationships. This is my favorite, and I retake the assessment every three years to see which of my themes have sharpened or weakened over time.

2. **Myers-Briggs Type Indicator (MBTI)**: This assessment groups you into one of sixteen personality types based on how you direct and receive energy, absorb information, make decisions, engage with people, your level of confidence, and your level of resistance to stress factors; 16Personalities.com is a free web-based assessment tool that uses the MBTI methodology.

3. **VIA Character Strengths Survey**: This assessment is focused on your inner values and character strengths rather than behavior, which can give insight into how you want to show up in the world.

4. **Insights Discovery**: This assessment uses color psychology to highlight key personality preferences and associated behaviors. This is particularly helpful if you want to understand your communication style and its impact on others.

These are helpful, but you may want to explore other options such as DiSC, the Enneagram, Hogan Development Survey, or Kolbe A Index.

Upon completing a questionnaire, you will receive a report with an in-depth analysis of your strengths, weakness, personality, or preferences as assessed by each tool's algorithms.

The reports provide specific language to communicate your preferences to others. Knowing your strengths is not enough; you need to utilize them in the proper context and communicate them to others.

These reports also provide direction on where your talents and personality will thrive and where they can be viewed as a weakness when misplaced or misappropriated, like my client Joanne. She is praised for being a disruptor in her community work fighting against human trafficking but labeled as disruptive when she raises issues in meetings at her corporate job. Such blind spots have the power to constrain or derail our good performance and image.

Of course, assessments are not without their limitations.

The conditions in which you take the assessment are very important. Conduct the evaluation when you have uninterrupted time to reflect and avoid being at the extremes of the emotional spectrum (too happy, too sad, too awake, or too tired). As discussed in Chapter Two, your feelings help you differentiate between your strengths and your super strengths. Consequently, as your feelings fluctuate, your assessment of your strengths could also vary.

Respond honestly rather than hopefully to the assessment statements. Often, we can subconsciously select answers that depict where we would like to be instead of where we are at present.

Consider this example of someone taking a strengths or personality assessment.

Bisi admires people that can connect with others and build relationships. Although it's not her natural talent or preference, her aspiration to develop this talent leads her to select "strongly agree" with the statements about her capacity to build relationships.

Statement: You enjoy meeting new people

Bisi's Answer: Strongly agree

Statement: When you enter a room, you are not shy to start the conversation

Bisi's Answer: Strongly agree

As a result, the assessment generates a report that says Relationship Building is one of Bisi's core strengths, which is incorrect. While these tools attempt to prevent such problems by asking the same question in different ways, there remains an inherent risk of generating an incorrect result because you haven't answered the question honestly.

Finally, research an assessment's methodology and the depth of insight before using it. Depending on what you want to discover about yourself, one assessment may be more appropriate than another. I have found it helpful to take two or three assessments to develop a more rounded picture of my strengths.

I do want to stress that while psychometric assessments can be helpful, they are not meant to define you or place you in a box. Ultimately, you know yourself more than anyone can, so listen to your instincts. Claim the talents that you recognize and value, and use them as the foundation for building an understanding of your strengths.

SEEKING EXTERNAL FEEDBACK

It can be helpful to consider input from people around you who might help you discover more strengths, validate or invalidate some of your findings, and shine a light on blind spots that you have. Family, friends, colleagues, mentors, coaches, and others can be a powerful source to gain more awareness of your strengths (as well as your areas of development).

I experienced the impact of seeking insights from others when I participated in a strengths coaching program in 2014. My coach asked me to choose three people—a friend, a family member, and a work colleague—who would give me their perspective by answering one question: What three words would you use to describe me and why?

I did, and about a week later, their responses arrived.

Beatrice, a friend

Passionate, diligent, and empowering

You're passionate and diligent about anything you put your hands on. You always give 250 percent to your education, job, and projects. You are determined to get the best result. You are also kind, friendly, generous with your time, and always keen to support and empower people.

Diana, a colleague at work

Confident, hardworking, and a helpful educator

Every time you walk into a room, you own it. You are unapologetic about your presence and ready to challenge the status quo. You work harder than anyone I know. Even when you are unwell, you still put in the hours just because you want to execute well. You have been so helpful at work and never seem to mind when I ask endless questions. You are always ready to draw your mind maps and walk me through things even when you are busy. The analysts on the team also talk about how invested you are in training them and how great you are at it.

Elizabeth, my mum

Determined, independent, and generous

You stopped breastfeeding at two months old and started using a feeding bottle. Before long, you were holding the bottle by yourself. I knew then that you were independent. While your cousins played, you would sit for hours doing homework, determined to finish it before playtime. As I have watched you grow up, your generosity stands out to me. You are ready to help people with your time and money even when it costs you everything.

As my coach and I assessed their responses, we looked for patterns by reviewing words that came up more than once, discussing whether any comments surprised me.

I was not surprised that hard work, diligence, and determination were consistently observed. However, I was surprised about how my responders all highlighted my passion for investing in and educating people. Using words like passionate, empowering, helpful educator, and generous, I realized that even my small, unconscious behaviors had made a significant impression on others.

The story goes that when I was three years old, I would stand in front of my primary school classroom and tell my teacher, "That is not how you do it. This is how it is done." Then I would go around helping my classmates to the point that the teacher would sarcastically hand me the chalk and invite me to teach the class. This continued in secondary school and university, where I would drop everything to help a classmate understand the lecture materials.

Although I pursued a career in finance, my love for learning and teaching never waned. I spent hours explaining concepts to new interns and analysts at work. I enjoyed the process of restructuring what I had learned to help others better understand concepts and principles. It energized me!

As I share this story, it feels obvious that educating was a natural talent, but at the time, I had taken it for granted. This process reconfirmed my sense of self and also helped me acknowledge talents that I was unaware of.

With this new awareness, my coach encouraged me to seek more ways to utilize this newly discovered talent in and out of the workplace. I did, and it was very well received. I became more intentional about sharing my knowledge of products, processes, and policies with my teammates and business partners. I started sending out regular emails and hosting information sessions about best practices and new regulations that everyone could benefit from.

I also volunteered to colead my department's graduate recruitment and training team, responsible for analysts' ongoing development. This role led me to join the global training team that trained new colleagues in credit risk fundamentals and internal risk processes every year at our head office in Charlotte, North Carolina. The more I leaned into this teaching talent, the sharper it became.

When I received written feedback that said, "Mary is a well-recognized and sought-after coach and mentor for her junior colleagues," I knew that my talent had developed into a super strength.

Outside of work, I've done the same. Through my social-first company, viSHEbility, I've gotten the opportunity to work with professionals, run workshops, and even write this book. I used to say, "If I were not a banker, I would be a teacher," until I realized that I did not have to choose. This proves that when something is a core strength, you can apply it in different environments to create and deliver value.

You may also have natural talents that are staring you in the face but have yet to be acknowledged. To help you get the same insight, find your three people and seek feedback by asking: What three words would you use to describe me and why?

Here are some alternative questions you can ask. Each one will shine a light on your talents from different angles.

1. What were your first impressions of me when we met?
2. What do you feel are my three best qualities?
3. What do you count on me for?
4. In what circumstances would you think about calling me first?
5. What kind of trip would you be planning for me to be invited?
6. Give me an example of when you perceived that I was operating at my best. What was I doing?
7. What do you think is meaningful to me?
8. What do you think is my intuitive style of problem solving?

Just like I did, you should select a mixture of people for this exercise, but what they should have in common is that they should be people who know you well and support you. They should be people you trust who will be honest with you and will not shy away from giving you difficult feedback.

You may feel some hesitation with asking for feedback. This is natural; it can be a pretty vulnerable and uncomfortable experience for both you and the giver, especially when areas of development need to be addressed. Here are some tips to help make the process less difficult for all parties.

- **Mindset**: Before you send your request, reframe your perspective on feedback being negative. You are doing more harm than good by staying ignorant about how others perceive you, what you do well, and where you need to improve.

- **Share your why**: Explain why you are seeking feedback and how it is crucial for your personal development (e.g., "I am working to define and communicate my strengths which I have often underestimated. I believe this would help me grow in my career").
- **Emphasize the relationship**: Be clear on why you have selected them specifically to contribute to this process (e.g., "I trust and respect your opinion, especially given your proximity to me and how I have observed you operating in your zone of strength in your career").
- **Encourage honesty and participation**: To avoid doubt, you should acknowledge that this may be uncomfortable for them and mention that you would like their feedback to be as unfiltered as possible (e.g., "This is a vulnerable request for me and may be an uncomfortable one for you. Nevertheless, please don't hold anything back. I will not take anything personally"). You can also encourage them to participate in the journey, asking them to provide tips for improving the areas of development they highlighted.
- **Leverage anonymity**: You can ask these questions via email or, better still, set up an anonymous questionnaire using tools like Typeform, Survey Monkey, or GetFeedback. Naturally, they may have concerns about how you would receive comments and the impact they may have on the relationship afterward. This is why offering the opportunity for anonymity is always appreciated and will typically encourage a more honest response.

YOUR TURN!

1. Psychometric Assessment: Take the *free* 16Personalities assessment at https://www.16personalities.com and analyze your results using the questions below.

Your Perceptions
- What was your first impression after reading your assessment report?
- Did any part of your report surprise you (e.g., strengths or weaknesses you were unaware of)?
- What words, phrases, or lines stood out to you in your report?
- Is there anything in your report that you disagree with?

Your Strengths in Action
- What strength do you recall applying in the past to get a successful result?
- Do you think people see your strengths in you?
- Considering your current or target role, how valuable do you think your strengths are for successfully executing your job?
- In what way(s) do you think you can intentionally use your strengths more personally, academically, or professionally?

2. Seeking Feedback from Others: Select three people (a friend, a family member, and a colleague).
- Using the template below, send an email asking them: What three words would you use to describe me?
- When their responses come in, look for patterns. What comes up consistently? What surprises you?

Template

Subject Line Ideas:
- *Your Insight Needed*
- *[YOUR NAME'S] Unique Abilities*
- *[THEIR NAME], what three words would you use to describe me?*

Hi [THEIR NAME]!

As part of my growth journey, I am working to define and communicate my strengths which I have often overlooked or underestimated.

I am reaching out to you as one of a select group of [friends/ family/colleagues] who I trust and respect to provide me with a bit of feedback.

I have one question: [What three words will you use to describe me and why?]

This is a vulnerable request for me and may be an uncomfortable one for you, but I want to make sure I understand how people perceive me. Please don't hold anything back. Remember that your feedback, however critical, will only help me grow.

Thank you so very much! I appreciate your help with this.

With much gratitude,

[YOUR NAME]

CHAPTER FOUR

Clarify What Matters

*"Hard work is painful when life is devoid of
purpose. But when you live for something greater
than yourself and the gratification of your own
ego, then hard work becomes a labor of love."*

—*Steve Pavlina*

****

Imagine getting up early, enduring the commute to the office,
sacrificing time with your family and friends, and working
countless hours for something you don't care about.

Sounds terrible, right? Sadly, when you don't take the time
to clarify what matters to you, you can end up in precisely
that position.

Clarifying what matters is about connecting your actions
to a reason and ensuring you understand why you do what
you do. In your career, you will have to decide what work
to do, where, when, and how to do it. Various factors and
people will influence those decisions, whether their influence

is solicited or unsolicited. Taking the time to clarify what matters to you will:

- Help you define success for yourself and reduce the urge to follow someone else's pathway
- Give you a focus toward which you can apply your strengths and prioritize your time
- Give meaning to your actions and the purpose of achieving something higher
- Facilitate optimal decision-making so you are less distracted by "shiny objects" that give you short-term satisfaction but don't align with what is most important to you

Overall, "finding purpose in your work will increase the long-term sense of satisfaction you feel in your life and improve your job effectiveness and engagement" (Tupper and Ellis, 2022).

HOW TO CLARIFY WHAT MATTERS

In clarifying what matters to you, you want to answer two specific questions.

What is my driving force or motivation?

This is the "why" for which you do what you do, the goal you are working to achieve, the problem you are trying to solve, and the alternate future you are working to create. The answer to this question is what keeps you going when times get challenging.

A recurring theme underpinning the success of many high-achieving individuals is their sense of purpose.

Whitney Wolfe Herd, the founder and CEO of the dating app Bumble, started the company because she wanted to "put women in control." The central focus of her app is that only women can initiate a conversation in heterosexual matches, preventing them from being bombarded with unwanted messages from men (BBC, 2021).

Kike Oniwinde, the cofounder of the Black Young Professionals (BYP) Network, started the company to "change the Black narrative." Through their platform, they connect over 150,000 Black professional members worldwide to niche local and global communities, job opportunities, up-skilling, employer Black networks, Black businesses, and other Black professionals (BYP Network, 2022).

This is not only true for business owners. Career professionals must also embody the same sense of purpose, just like Dr. Brown working on healthcare accessibility, Rolake with the provision of energy infrastructure, or Dr. Damilola leading skincare scientific direction in Africa. Each has clear internal or external drivers that provide a sense of direction, guide their career choices, and give meaning to their work.

What are the life rules, principles, or values that guide my behavior?

Motivational speaker and life coach Tony Robbins defines values as the "fundamental beliefs that govern our lives.

They are our inspiration to act, and they guide our decisions about everything from career to personal growth. They embody the person we want to be, influencing how we treat others and how we interact with the world. Values are the core of who we are."

These rules can include excellence, integrity, respect, equality, justice, fairness, loyalty, wealth, authority, influence, and many more. They serve as an internal check that helps you make choices you are comfortable with.

Every life rule has two sides. Elizabeth is a creative director and has loyalty as a life rule. She is supportive of anyone who has earned her loyalty. While this is admirable, she often finds herself unable to leave situations and relationships that have become toxic and do not deserve her loyalty.

If you already embody a strong sense of purpose and clarity on your life rules that grounds you, that's terrific! But for many individuals, these are questions that one can spend a lifetime trying to answer.

I want to offer you three steps to clarify what matters to you.

STEP 1: INTROSPECTION

Your view of what matters to you—your why and how—forms from childhood through adulthood. When you were born you were a blank canvas, and with each day your experiences leave a mark on the canvas that colors the lens through which you view the future.

To understand why you do what you do and the way you do it, you need to look inward to examine your thoughts and emotions. In particular, you need a clearer picture of how your experiences have shaped your thinking and approach.

What matters to you could be observed in the following areas.

1. Your childhood upbringing and what you observed around you

"Make sure you leave it better than you met it," is a mantra I grew up hearing my parents say from about the age of four. Their life ethos was to leave every person, place, and process better than they met it. They instilled this in me through repetition, behavior modeling, and enforcing compliance.

This occurred in the small things, like tidying up after myself when I finished playing. If I didn't, I would hear my mum shout, "Is that how you met it? Go back and make sure it's better than you met it, young lady." But it also occurred in the big things, like my parents being on steering committees in our church and the local community. When I had the opportunity to observe them in these meetings, I saw them challenge and express strong views of how things could and must be improved. When we had new home staff, my parents took the time to teach them and expose them to a new way of doing things. They provided financial support and connected new staff to their network of benefactors that could be of further help.

"Make sure you leave it better than you met it" was not just a slogan. It guided their personal and professional choices. Despite having fantastic opportunities to work in the lucrative private sector in their respective fields, my parents took lower-paying public sector jobs because they believed there was ample opportunity to improve things, which they did. Their efforts were rewarded by career growth and deep satisfaction.

In 1994, they were publicly awarded the chieftaincy titles Taiyese and Yeye Taiyese of Lagos, Nigeria, where they lived and worked. Taiyese is Yoruba for "Reformer," so their titles in English were Reformer and Wife of Reformer—very appropriate for them.

I had a front-row seat to the life of these exceptional individuals who influenced me to adopt the same. My ethos is everyday leadership. I believe that ordinary people become extraordinary leaders because we choose to be part of the solution in every sphere we are in. I was taught to be the change and elevated that to leading the change. Similar to my parents, this rule of life guides my behavior.

At work and in my many endeavors, I constantly look for gaps to fill and I get bored in spaces where change cannot happen. I always think, *How can I make this—people, processes, products, or places—better than before I stepped on the scene?* I then take the next step to lead the change that I want to see.

I recognize that some of your childhood lessons may not necessarily be positive and could be lessons that have developed into limiting beliefs impacting you negatively. Later, I will share helpful tips on replacing these limiting beliefs with more empowering ones.

Ask yourself these key questions:

- What lessons were reinforced in my childhood that now govern my life?
- What behaviors did I see in my childhood that I now want to model in adulthood?

- How does my upbringing influence my choice of work and how I want to show up in my career?

2. The obstacles you have faced and the places you want to have a significant impact

Often, very painful experiences can create either desperation to run as far away from the problems that caused the pain, or a deep desire to solve those same problems.

Thasunda Brown Duckett is the CEO of Teachers Insurance and Annuity Association of America (TIAA), a leading provider of secure retirements and outcome-focused investment solutions to millions of people and thousands of institutions. She is the fourth Black woman to serve as a Fortune 500 CEO. Thasunda credits much of her success to finding her career passion for personal finance early on.

"When you know what it's like to look in the refrigerator and just see baking soda or know what it's like to have your lights turned off, personal finance is important," she explained in an interview with *New York Times* (CNBC, 2021). The inequities she observed as a young girl led her to start her career leading affordable housing initiatives for people of color at mortgage loan company Fannie Mae in 1996.

In 2021, when she was announced CEO of TIAA, she reflected on the importance of the full-circle moment. "I often think about the day my father asked me to help him plan his retirement, and I had to tell him, 'Dad, your pension is not enough.' . . . I am extraordinarily grateful for the opportunity to lead a company that has helped millions of people retire with enough to live in dignity (CNBC, 2021). I am excited about the opportunity to help TIAA chart its next one hundred years."

Thasunda has spent all of her career in various areas of consumer finance, aligning her deepest pains with her work. You can also align your work with a deep desire to solve the problems that you or those close to you have faced. Turn your pain into passion.

Ask yourself these key questions:

- What problem do I want to be part of solving?
- What do I want to be remembered for?
- How do I want to contribute to humanity and society?
- How do my negative experiences influence my choice of where I want to work and how I want to show up in my career?

3. The role models who inspire you

Inspiration is so powerful. When we are inspired, we are filled with a sense of necessity and excitement, new possibilities that we would not have recognized on our own are revealed, and we are energized to pursue more important and larger goals (Thrash and Elliot, 2003).

Kike Sanyaolu is a chartered architect working as a design manager at Galliford Try, a construction company. With her father and close uncles being architects, Kike's initial interest in architecture was environmentally induced. Reflecting on her career path, she said, "I spent much time in my father's practice among the firm's architects. I was exposed to creation, and the beauty of architecture caught my attention. I knew I wanted to be in that field."

Kike later decided to study for her bachelor's degree and master's in architecture at the University of Liverpool, England. She then completed her diploma qualification at the University College London and became a member of the Royal Institute of British Architects and the Chartered Institute of Builders. Despite a grueling academic journey, Kike remained resilient.

"I knew going into architecture that my journey from starting my undergraduate degree to getting my professional qualifications was seven years. I knew I didn't want an incomplete journey, so that kept me focused. I wanted to reach the peak of what I was trying to achieve. At every turning point, every graduation, I just kept thinking, 'I'm not there yet.'"

Midway through her studies, she spent a three-month summer holiday on a work placement with an architecture firm. "I got a placement in central London. It was unpaid, but the value could not be estimated. I knew that with this experience, I would return to university with more confidence, refined practical perspective, and new role models."

Role models are great at helping you see a real vision of a potential future and provide a blueprint for the career you want to build. Kike stayed inspired, and that kept her grounded.

Ask yourself these key questions:

- Who inspires me, who doesn't, and why?

- What did I see myself doing as a child before I knew fear?
- How do my role models influence my choice of where I want to work and how I want to show up in my career?

This list is not exhaustive but should be a helpful prompt for your introspection.

STEP 2: VISUALIZATION

Could you build a jigsaw puzzle without looking at the picture on the box? Without the image on the box, you'd aimlessly try to force pieces together with no clue what you're doing.

This analogy, explained by executive leadership coach Cynthia Corsetti in her review of Eric C. Sinoway and Merrill Meadow's book *Howard's Gift*, speaks to the power of visualization in creating mental pictures of the outcomes you want to achieve in your career. It allows you to see and feel your future success before it happens.

A creative way of visualizing is through something called the Press Release exercise. One of my friends, Michelle Marbie Davies, who is excellent at business branding, asked me to do this during a viSHEbility branding session.

The exercise was challenging, but the results were instrumental in helping me clarify what I wanted to do with the company. I now routinely ask the women I coach to do this exercise, which has been pivotal in unlocking some significant transformations.

Your mission is to develop a short press release that you would want to see about yourself in a leading newspaper or online magazine in ten years. Wherever the feature is, it's giving you great coverage and includes details of your career, including where you work or the business(es) you run and what you have achieved.

You must include these key points:

1. Who you are and what your brand represents
2. What you specialize in or what you're known for
3. What you are doing that is grabbing everyone's attention at the time (ten years from now)

You can also include important life details such as where you live, key people, relationships, and social status.

This exercise will force you to consider what achievements you want to be associated with at crucial moments in your life.

Take Anna-Noémie Ouattara Boni for example. Anna was a student in the first cohort of my career accelerator program. Here is her press release submission.

> *Anna-Noémie is an Ivorian entrepreneur and leader. She's an expert in financial inclusion, a chartered accountant, and a certified wealth and financial planner with over ten years of experience. Through her diverse and unique experiences, Anna-Noémie has been featured in the Forbes 30 under 30 in 3 categories—Finance, Social impact, and Education. This young lady from Abidjan*

has positively contributed to bettering more than five
thousand lives across West African communities through
her development projects with her charity WinORG. It
would interest you to know that Anna-Noémie is also
behind the successful coffee and smoothie bars, providing
innovative hospitality services in Abidjan. Anna-Noémie
aspires to build better and resilient communities through
connected high experience with finance and development.

The specificity and diversity of Anna's press release stood out to me. She knew what areas of society she wanted to impact and how she wanted to do it. She also included other interests like owning a bar, a testament to the fact that we can all be multifaceted even in our vision casting.

The challenge, however, was that when Anna wrote this, she was working as a wealth and personal banking graduate at HSBC. She was unfulfilled in her job, but like many young professionals, Anna had been conditioned to be grateful that she even had a job and not rock the boat. Her unhappiness led her to me. I could immediately see that her dissatisfaction stemmed from the fact that she was spending more than ten hours a day in a job that did not fuel the career vision she was silently nurturing in her heart.

Seeing her vision statement on paper marked a turning point for Anna. Here was a tangible reminder that she was not where she needed to be if she genuinely wanted to get where she wanted to go, a reminder of what standing still was costing her. Putting her vision into words was like putting a mirror to her face, and when she didn't like what she saw, she decided to do something about it.

You can also paint a beautiful picture of the future you desire through deep questioning.

Ask yourself the following questions:

- What do I want my life to look like in five or ten years?
- What do I want out of a career?
- Who do I want to become?
- What is important to me?
- What do I want to accomplish?
- Who do I want to have in my life? What role do I want work to play in my life?
- What does the entire picture look like when I visualize it?

At best, the answers to these questions will help you draw a road map. At worst, they will highlight a dislocation and force you to redirect your steps.

STEP 3: EXPLORATION

As you introspect your past and visualize your future, ensure you don't do it in a vacuum. Research, immersive exploration of your interests, and ultimately decision-making are vital to clarify what matters to you.

After writing her press release, Anna was much more aware that having a career in the development space was important to her. Her next step was to start researching and exploring the field more actively. She identified some programs at the United Nations and World Bank organizations she wanted to access. She sought out a few people in those programs to gain their perspectives and advice on how to apply successfully.

When she realized that a critical application criterion was a master's qualification, Anna decided that her best course of action was to take a year out of work and return to school to pursue a master's in the political economy of development, stating, "This year out will allow me to clarify what I want to do in this broad development space. I want to dive into the theory of development so that I can better articulate my passion." Anna completed her master's program and was offered a long-term internship with the United Nations Development Program (UNDP).

Similarly, you should seek immersive experiences that can offer you practical insight into the work you want to do. Consider further studies, job shadowing, taking on internships, and other part-time work. You may have heard the saying that "all that glitters is not gold." Seeking practical academic and professional experiences within your areas of interest will help you make informed decisions without rose-tinted glasses on.

For example, if companies are named in your press release, go to their website and look around. Figure out all the different types of jobs available and the skills required. Read about the people who work there and what they do daily. Now that you know a bit more, does it still excite you?

While it may seem that Anna wasted the first two years of her career in a job she wasn't satisfied with, she gained some transferable skills and made connections that will serve her throughout her career. Furthermore, she gained insight into what she did not like, which is a helpful data point and reason enough to explore her options.

Recognizing what you don't want by critically looking at every experience you have and asking, "How did this make me feel? How did this grow me? Do I want to do more or less of it?" can be easier than discerning what you do want. If you make each experience a teachable moment in your career journey, you will realize that nothing is a waste of time.

Clarifying what matters was Anna's springboard to the career of her dreams. It can be the same for you!

IT TAKES TIME

As I reflect on my career so far, I see how my career vision was birthed in stages.

My role models inspired me to consider a career in accounting, and my natural analytical skills and curiosity for commerce helped me in my accounting and finance studies. My internships helped me explore my career options, leading me to a risk management career. My years of experience in banking grew my awareness of how impactful access to credit can be for businesses of all sizes, which has fueled my passion even more. The mentors and leaders I have worked for have inspired me to stay in finance and see it as an enabling environment for many other interests, such as gender, racial, and socioeconomic equity in the workplace.

Even my faith has been an anchor in my career. In 2014, in a season when I was very unsure of what direction I was going, I remember reading my Bible and stumbling upon Deuteronomy 28:12 (New Living Translation):

The Lord will send rain at the proper time from his rich treasury in the heavens and will bless all the work you do. You will lend to many nations, but you will never need to borrow from them.

This was a heavenly message! My job was literally to lend to companies providing funding for operational, liquidity, and strategic needs. I instinctively felt that I was in the right place.

Even if you don't believe in God, I believe the universe is constantly working to get our attention. It directs us down the right path if we are present, open, and willing to receive answers. That being said, what matters to you will evolve as you evolve. With age, experience, and exposure, our priorities shift. For some people, the shifts are small but consistent changes. For others, they are big swings. Either way, changing is okay. In fact, expect your *why* to change, because you can only make decisions based on the information and exposure you have at the time. Don't shy away from taking the first step because of fear that you will get it wrong. There really is no wrong.

I have worked diligently and intensely in finance for the last fifteen years. However, I have always straddled my functional role with work in diversity and inclusion, recruitment, training, and people development. I never set out to build my professional career in this area, but the more I did it, my experience and passion grew. I knew I had to integrate all facets of my being into my vision because it deeply matters to me.

Today, I am a risk manager and a social entrepreneur, and I have learned to leverage skills adopted in one sphere to another. My coaching and advocacy skills learned through building and running my business make me a better people manager and culture reformer at work. My analytical and leadership skills learned in banking help me run my business effectively, raise capital, and lead a team of high-performing individuals.

In clarifying what matters, be patient with yourself. As poet and author Maggie Smith said, "Even if you don't believe you have 'purpose,' think about the work you can do in the world that would make a difference to others. What art can you make, what comfort can you bring, what wrong can you set right? If you can do it, you should do it."

YOUR TURN!

1. Introspection: go through this chapter and answer the key questions in each sub-section.
2. Visualization: craft your ten-year press release.
3. Exploration: write three practical ways you will research and explore your interests.

CHAPTER FIVE

Manifest Your Vision

"A vision without a strategy remains an illusion."

—Lee Bolman

****

Think of the last time you set out to achieve something for yourself. How did you go about it? Did you jump in with your feet first, or did you spend time thinking, planning, and setting goals?

Even when you have clarified what matters to you, getting there may still feel intangible, unattainable, and overwhelming. For this reason, you need to break the big picture into smaller actionable objectives, often known as goals.

Goal setting is subject to some pretty polarizing views. Some people demonize it with claims that when you set goals, you may be limiting your ability to take spontaneous decisions in your life—such as moving countries, changing careers, or learning a new skill—if they don't fit into your well-crafted plans. Others view the process of goal setting as unjustifiably time-consuming with the effect of sucking you into endless hours of plotting and planning rather than doing.

While these potential downsides to goal setting are undeniable, research shows that having goals increases our motivation, commitment, effort, and performance (Locke and Latham, 2006).

In my own life, I have seen the power of setting goals in various areas where I wanted to see change and progress, notably in my academics, finances, business, fitness, and career. Rather than limiting or paralyzing me, I found that setting goals helped me lay out what steps and support I needed in order to get to where I wanted. They provided me with a sense of satisfaction as I achieved each milestone on the journey. They also motivated me to carry on as life threw curve balls and distractions my way.

But is goal setting all it takes? I wish it were.

Many women I have mentored come to me with goals such as securing a new job or promotion. Often, they have had the goal for a while but were unsuccessful in hitting their markers. They had defined the why and the what but not the how. They had not created systems that aligned their behavior, decisions, and activities with their goals. These systems are known as strategy.

In 2016, I sustained an injury to my knee, which impacted my mobility. Coupled with months of poor diet choices, I put on some unwanted weight and reached my heaviest at eighty-five kilograms. I still looked good, but I noticed that

I struggled to do things like climbing stairs, walking, or bending down. My clothes had also become tighter and even unwearable. For someone who was always quite athletic, this was not a state of health that was acceptable to me. I resolved to lose the weight.

I did some online research and started my journey with intermittent fasting and working out six days a week. Two months later, I was on my third meal plan and barely managed to complete one workout session a week. The busier work and life became, the harder it was for me to keep up.

As I considered giving up, I stumbled upon a billboard showcasing some amazing before and after pictures for clients of a body transformation gym. I was inspired by what I saw and went to check them out. A few weeks later, I signed up.

The first thing they asked me to do was to fill out a client questionnaire:

1. What is your target weight? If possible, share an image of someone with your ideal physique.
2. When do you want to achieve this target?
3. Beyond losing weight, what would it mean to achieve your body transformation goal?
4. Have you embarked on a body transformation journey before and failed? What do you think you did wrong?
5. Are you in the right environment and around the right people to help you on your journey?
6. Do you agree to attend all workout sessions and follow your coach's exercise and dietary guidance?

As I answered the questions, I realized that the objective of these questions was to help me set goals and implement an effective strategy.

Setting a target weight of seventy kilograms and providing an image as a blueprint helped me define what success looked like for me. I also used my thirtieth birthday in five months as the target date to achieve my transformation. Both these factors gave the gym administrators what they needed to pair me with an ideal coach.

My coach and I agreed on a twenty-four-week transformation plan. We selected my food options and decided on the frequency of my exercises in and out of the gym. We also set reminders for when I needed to submit my food logs, measurements, and body profile pictures so we could record how my body was changing during the journey.

I found meaningful motivation in considering the deeper meaning behind achieving my goal. I come from a family with a history of weight-related diseases, so I also wanted to create a value system of healthy living to break the cycle of health challenges in my family.

By reflecting on my past failures and environment, I could identify the limiting beliefs, unhelpful habits, and unsupportive people that hindered my progress. I committed to taking actions that would improve my chances of success, such as throwing out junk food, scheduling time to prepare healthy meals for the week, logging my meals, and joining a community of others trying to achieve a similar goal.

Finally, by using a coach and agreeing to follow his guidance, I created a system of accountability to ensure I stayed on the right track. First, the program was at a considerable cost, so I knew I couldn't afford to skip sessions or be unserious about it. Second, the biweekly check-in points kept me honest because we all know that numbers don't lie and a picture is worth a thousand words.

By week twenty-four, I was down to sixty-nine kilograms, exceeding my goals. I could do it because I had clear goals and an effective strategy that guided and encouraged me to do the necessary work. Goal setting was important, but strategy made the difference.

It has been five years since that process, and I have maintained my weight, proving that when a strategy is effective, its results are long-lasting and repeatable.

The same is true for your career. Manifesting the vision of your career involves the continuous process of analyzing your strengths and clarifying what matters, setting "good" goals, and implementing an effective strategy that places you on the right track toward your intention.

CAREER GOALS THAT WILL TAKE YOU FAR

Whether you are coming into the job market for the first time, switching industries, or growing where you are, having goals will help you identify the short- to medium-range actions that together help you achieve your long-range vision.

Suppose a recent graduate in mechanical engineering living in Ghana had ambitions to be CEO of a Fortune 500 Technology company in North America. Their associated short-range goals—that is, goals that are achievable within a year—could look like this:

- Read *The Economist* every week to improve my knowledge of the world of business
- Research the pathway to CEO by listening to podcast interviews of CEOs of tech companies

Their associated medium-range goals, which require at least a few years to accomplish, could look like this:

- In three years, I will embark on an executive MBA program at Harvard to improve my knowledge, expand my network, and open me up to opportunities to relocate to North America
- After my MBA, I will secure a job in the business development function of a Fortune 500 company so I can learn how to market and grow a business
- After two years, I will move to the operations division so I can expand my portfolio and strengthen my execution skills by delivering satisfactory projects on time and within budget

Goals don't necessarily have to depend on time. You can categorize them into different types as well. These include but are not limited to performance goals, learning and experience goals, relationship goals, visibility goals, progression goals, earning goals, and giving goals.

PERFORMANCE GOALS

These goals relate to the problems you want to solve and how you will do it.

Consistent strong performance is the entry ticket in the workplace, ensuring you land in a position to demand what you want. Having performance goals will ensure that you are focused on demonstrating your capabilities and your capacity to execute on strategic and operational priorities. Consider these questions:

- What low-functioning work processes can I take the lead on improving?
- What stretch projects or assignments can I take on?
- What training can I provide to help others perform better?

LEARNING AND EXPERIENCE GOALS

These goals relate to your personal and professional development.

Whether entering the job market for the first time, switching industries, taking on a new stretch project, or seeking a promotion, you will likely need to close the gap between your current skills and abilities and what you require for what you are trying to achieve. Having goals for your learning and experiences will help you be intentional about identifying and closing your skills gaps. Consider these questions:

- What skills do I have today?

- What skills do I need for where I want to go?
- How can I close those skills gaps?

As a worker in today's economy, you need to think not only about the job you do but about the bundle of skills you have. Try new things that may seem off the beaten path. The knowledge you gain will come in handy at some point, or at a minimum, it will widen your perspective and give you an experience to remember.

RELATIONSHIP GOALS

These goals relate to the connections you want to make and relationships you want to foster.

Since organizations are a collection of people, relationships with others are fundamental to how you ideate, execute, and progress at work. Having relationship goals will ensure you are both tactical and strategic about connecting with key players along your trajectory. Consider these questions:

- Who are those that are critical to my performance, learning, and progression?
- Where are they located, and how will I connect with them? What communities or interest groups do they belong to, what projects are they part of, and if they are not local, how can I visit them?

This strategy was game-changing for me. Following my promotion to vice president at BoA, I set a goal to deepen my global relationships and take on more strategic projects to increase my visibility at the start of the year. I knew that spending some time at our head office in Charlotte, North Carolina, would be a solid strategic move since many key decision-makers were there. I travelled to Charlotte from London to work there for two weeks.

While there, I met many of the senior leaders I had heard about or spoken to. I also met some important project leads and spent time understanding their goals and how I could contribute to their work. Meeting in person helped deepen those connections and opened the door to opportunities I may otherwise not have had.

Ultimately, people hire and promote those they know, like, and trust, and you can benefit from that by focusing on your relationships.

VISIBILITY GOALS

These goals relate to how you intend to make yourself physically identifiable and connected with the work that you are doing and the results you are generating.

In the busyness of work, rolling through your list of tasks without thinking about how you share your work with those who need to know about it is too easy. Having visibility goals will ensure you are prioritizing the critical work of advertising yourself and your work. Consider these questions:

- What have I done, and why have I done it?
- Who is directly impacted by the work that I am doing?
- How do I let these people know how my work can be helpful to them?

PROGRESSION GOALS

These goals relate to how you want to grow your career within and beyond your current role.

Progression goals ensure you consider how you want to expand your portfolio and your responsibilities. For example, you may feel ready to start leading a project or managing people. Having progression goals will keep you focused on the necessary work and remind you to keep communicating your expectations with key decision-makers. Consider these questions:

- Where am I on the career ladder now?
- What will it take to get to the next level?
- Who do I need to communicate my intentions to, and whose support do I need?

EARNING GOALS

These goals relate to how you want compensation for your time and effort and the value you deliver.

Having earning goals will ensure that your compensation does not stagnate. It also encourages you to be aware of all the steps and people involved in the decisions around your pay. Consider these questions:

- How does my pay compare to my peers in similar organizations?
- When are decisions about compensation made, and who are the key decision-makers?
- Besides pay, is there any other worthwhile thing I can request (e.g., education or professional sponsorship,

additional vacation days, flexible working arrange-
ments, pension top-up, company shares, etc.)?

GIVING GOALS

These goals relate to how you want to help other people.

An empty life only feeds itself and has no consideration for
others. I have found that when I help others, I, in turn, find
the help I am seeking. This is how the law of sowing and
reaping works. Consider these questions:

- Who am I going to support this year?
- Who am I going to mentor?
- Who am I going to recommend for opportunities?

SETTING "GOOD" GOALS

Setting the right goal is very important, but crafting those
goals correctly can mean the difference between success
and failure.

In 1981, George Doran, Arthur Miller, and James Cunning-
ham coined the SMART framework for setting goals. They
said that for goals to be effective, they must be Specific,
Measurable, Assignable, Realistic, and Time-related. Over
the years, thought leaders have substituted and expanded
the framework to suit various focus areas.

I have adapted and expanded the framework to SMARTER
to focus on how to set career goals. As you break your wider
vision down into smaller goals, your goals should be Specific,

Motivational, Accountable, Realistic, Time-bound, Exciting, and Relevant.

SPECIFIC

Your goals should feel tangible and well-defined. What are you working toward?

- **Instead of:** I want to "level up" in the new year.
- **Say/Do:** I want to return to school. I want to ask for a pay rise. I want to lose weight. I want to buy a house.

MOTIVATIONAL

Your goals should demand something from you. They should be far-reaching and call forth a better and greater you to achieve them. Your goals must motivate better choices and improved behavior. They must want to make you learn and grow.

- **Instead of:** I want to work on more projects.
- **Say/Do:** Next year, I want to work on a cross-geographical regulatory project so I can learn more about

regulatory frameworks and build my network of international colleagues.

ACCOUNTABLE

Specificity is a solid start, but it's missing something important: numbers. Quantifying your goals makes it easier to measure progress and verify its completion.

- **Instead of:** I want to earn more.
- **Say/Do:** I want to increase my income by 50 percent by December 2022.

REALISTIC

Your goals should take into account the results that you can achieve given the resources that you have available or that are accessible to you. While your goals should be aspirational, they should also exist in the realm of possibility given you do the necessary work.

- **Instead of:** I want to change careers in one month.
- **Say/Do:** Set a timeframe that feels more reasonable. Complete the smaller tasks between where you are and where you want to go, such as assessing your skills gaps, identifying role models, up-skilling, and finding the role you wish to apply for.

TIME-BOUND

Your goals should have a time frame within which you would like to achieve them.

- **Instead of:** I want to change jobs.
- **Say/Do:** I want to change jobs to X industry or company by December 31, 2022.

EXCITING

Your goals should excite you. Remember when we talked about your strengths being the things that make you feel FINE? Your goals should also inspire excitement when you think about working toward them.

- **Instead of:** I want to take on more projects.
- **Say/Do:** I want to take on projects in product architecture because I feel fulfilled, interested, natural, and excited when I work in this area.

RELEVANT

Since your goals are a breakdown of your big picture vision, they should be relevant to the vision that you have for yourself. If you cannot identify how a specific goal contributes to the attainment of the vision, then that goal is irrelevant.

- **Instead of:** I am taking a course in shoe design.
- **Say/Do:** I am taking a course in shoe design because I want to start my shoe brand in twelve months.

EFFECTIVE STRATEGY

In 2007, professor of psychology at Dominican University Dr. Gail Matthews conducted a study on achieving goals. Her conclusions found that individuals who wrote down their goals, committed to taking action, and had a robust system of accountability were almost twice more likely to achieve their goals than those who stopped at just thinking about the goals they wanted to accomplish.

These three steps are the fundamental elements of an effective strategy.

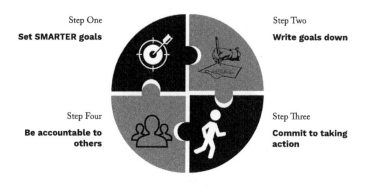

Step One
Set SMARTER goals

Step Two
Write goals down

Step Four
Be accountable to others

Step Three
Commit to taking action

WRITING GOALS DOWN

In his *Forbes* article titled, "Neuroscience explains why you need to write down your goals if you actually want to achieve them," Mark Murphy, founder of LeadershipIQ.com and *New York Times* best-selling author, explains that this is critical for the following reasons:

1. **Record keeping and external storage:** Since you cannot rely on your brain to remember everything, writing down your goals helps to free up your mental space and makes it easier to access and review. You can write it

down on paper, type it on a computer, or create a vision board.

2. **Visual cue:** Being able to stare at your goals can serve as a much-needed reminder when life gets busy or when you are about to make choices that are not in alignment with your goals.

3. **Encoding and improved recollection:** Writing improves the brain's encoding process and increases the probability of remembering the things you have written down.

COMMITMENT TO ACT

For all the people whose stories I have shared in this book, including myself, through our fears, discomfort, and spiraling questions, we had one thing in common: we decided to act, knowing that only action (not intent) can make things happen.

You need to take the best action with the information, mindset, and exposure you have. Taking action is what brings the clarity you are seeking. It helps you understand which pathways are viable and which are not. It lets you know where more or less work is needed and lets you map out what logical steps come next.

What does a commitment to action look like? It means deciding to take daily steps toward your goals. It doesn't matter how small your actions are or how slow you think you are progressing. You will get closer to success if you keep going.

Differentiate between motivation and commitment as the driver of your actions. Motivation is the inspiration and desire to get something done. It serves as the starting point, but it can only get you so far.

Commitment, on the other hand, "is both an internal desire plus a cognitive decision that is combined with specific, tangible action" (Rao, 2019). Many of us desire to change, but we are not committed to making it happen. Commitment means making a plan and sticking to it. It means not abandoning your goal when you hit an obstacle. Commitment requires hard work and sacrifice. It may mean waking up early, sacrificing free time and money, getting uncomfortable with the unknown, and taking risks. Commitment means doing things you may not want to do because you know it will yield the desired results.

ACCOUNTABILITY

Setting SMARTER goals makes it more likely that you will reach your goals, but we're all human. We can get busy, tired, make excuses, get confused, lose motivation, and get off track. Therefore, we need people to help keep us accountable.

How much more effective would your process be if you had someone asking you if you have done the research, applied for that job, asked for a promotion or pay raise, or booked your ticket for that conference you have been meaning to attend for years?

Accountability partners will help you set milestones, ask how you are progressing, and give you tough love when needed. They can provide assistance, recommendations or referrals, and sometimes even funding. They can be your friends, family, mentors, work colleagues, and even bosses. If you can afford to, you may also want to seek out someone who provides a service professionally, like a career coach.

Whoever you decide to have as your accountability partner should be someone you trust with your goals and who can act as your conscience when life gets in the way. They must have the time to regularly ask you how things are going and be able to do what is necessary to keep you from quitting. They should also be there to celebrate your wins with you because they genuinely care about you and the outcomes you are striving for.

Time and time again, I have seen the value of implementing these three elements of effective strategy in achieving goals, like with Funmi, an engineer working in financial services.

For about three years, Funmi had a goal to relocate countries for work. When we started working together in February 2018, Funmi had become disillusioned about the prospect, and her excitement was waning. From our first call, we established that the biggest obstacle to accomplishing her goal was that she had not set good goals and did not have an effective strategy to keep her on track.

To get the ball rolling again, I asked Funmi to do four things.

1. **Redraft her goal to make it SMARTER:**
   - **Problem:** Her goal was not specific or time-bound.
   - **Change:** Her goal evolved from "I want to relocate countries" to "I want to relocate from the London

office to the Paris office of my existing company by December 2018."

- **Impact:** By getting specific on the city and country she wanted to move to and her preference to remain with her current company, her efforts became more targeted. She focused on internal mobility opportunities in Paris rather than all opportunities in any company and country. Secondly, by selecting a date by which she wanted to move, Funmi was removing optionality from the process and giving herself a deadline toward which she would channel her efforts.

2. **Write down her goal where she could see it:**
   - **Problem:** Funmi's job kept her so busy that she often forgot about her intention to relocate.
   - **Change:** Funmi created a vision board with everything she loved about Paris. She set this as her phone and laptop screen saver. She also wrote down why she believed moving to Paris was good for her career.
   - **Impact:** Whenever she picked up one of her devices, the vision board reminded her that Paris was still in the plan.

3. **Commit to taking action:**
   - **Problem:** Funmi had not taken any relevant steps toward making Paris possible.
   - **Change:** Funmi and I created an extensive list of actions she needed to execute by specific dates.
     - Search the company intranet for available opportunities in Paris (March).

- Speak to the Human Resources manager covering the Paris office to indicate interest in internal mobility opportunities (March).
- Refresh my CV so that my experience and achievements are up to date (March).
- Enroll in French classes (April).
- Use the internal directory and LinkedIn to find colleagues in the engineering department in the Paris office and make a connection (March–May).
- Explore whether there are any projects I can get involved in with the Paris team so they can see how I deliver value (April–June).
- Take a short trip to Paris during which I can work in the Paris office (May).
- Research the immigration rules for France (June).
- Apply for an open position once one becomes available.

- **Impact:** Funmi realized that there was much to be done if she wanted to position and prepare herself for this transition. She acknowledged that she would merely continue wishing for the international move if she didn't take any action.

4. **Accountability:**
   - **Problem:** Funmi had shared that she wanted an international assignment with a few close people, but she had not explicitly tasked them with keeping her accountable.
   - **Change:** Funmi spoke with her father, her close friend, and one of her career mentors about her

goal. She shared her list of actions and committed to calling each of them every two weeks to give an update on her progress. She also permitted them to follow up if they did not hear from her. Additionally, she had me as her coach asking for a progress update on the action items during each session.

- **Impact:** Funmi did not want to disappoint her accountability partners, so she was doubly motivated to ensure that she was executing those action items. She also had a group of people partnering with her on the journey. We gave her advice, connected her with people we knew could be helpful, and pushed her when needed.

Result: Success!

Funmi connected with her colleagues and the HR manager in Paris via email. To deepen those relationships, Funmi flew to attend an industry conference in Paris, which allowed her to meet her colleagues in person for the first time.

During lunch, one of them saw her phone screen saver and struck up a conversation about it. "I would love to live and work in Paris by the end of the year," Funmi said to Adelaide, who happened to be the hiring manager for one of the fastest-growing product groups in Paris. Funmi stayed in touch with Adelaide via emails and phone calls.

Four months later, Adelaide had an opening on her team for a product design engineer at an appropriate level for Funmi's experience and asked Funmi to submit her CV. Within two weeks, Funmi started the interview process, and in October, she secured a role in the Paris office of her company to begin in January 2019. However, because of work permit delays, she started working remotely from London and then relocated in March 2019. She put in the work, and she accomplished her goal.

You can implement the same for any goal you are working to accomplish. Whether securing a new role within your organization, switching careers, asking for expanded responsibilities, asking for a pay raise or promotion, or relocating, if you apply these steps, you will multiply your chances of accomplishing your goal.

A WORD OF CAUTION: STAY FLEXIBLE

As human beings, we have so much capacity, but one thing we cannot do is predict the future. I must spell out that even if you have SMARTER goals and an effective strategy, not all plans will succeed. You will not always get the job, the promotion, or other opportunities you want, because those decisions are not solely in your hands.

As ex-COO of Meta, Sheryl Sandberg said, "Careers are not ladders [. . .] but jungle gyms." They are not limited to up or down moves but are full of false starts, detours, occasional dips, and dead ends. Unfortunately, while we should be using these experiences as stepping-stones, many of us let them demotivate us.

I have mentored early career professionals who became discouraged when they started exploring career possibilities and hit the first of many hurdles, like not getting the job they wanted or finding out that what they got was not what they expected.

Knowing the opportunities you will or will not secure or even what your priorities will be a few years from now is impossible. This should not deter you from planning, but it does mean that you should maintain an experimental mindset and a flexible disposition to your goal setting and strategy.

From the age of ten, I envisioned being an accountant. Throughout my academics, I selected courses that served as little stones on my journey to that goal. I had my eyes on working for one of the "Big 4" Accounting Firms—PricewaterhouseCoopers, Ernst & Young, Deloitte, and KPMG. However, when I started exploring work experience opportunities in my second year of university, I could not secure an accounting internship. This led me to my first internship in investment banking at Deutsche Bank. The year after, I tried to secure accounting opportunities again, but I was still unsuccessful. Something just didn't click with them, and I could not figure out why.

After much advice and searching, I got another internship as a portfolio manager at BoA in London. I planned to complete the three-month program and return to university to complete my master's degree. To my surprise, I loved it, and it loved me back! At the end of the internship, I secured a full-time graduate position to return after I completed my master's. It turned out to be a win-win. Imagine if I had not accepted the internship because I was stuck on a career in accounting?

Notwithstanding, I didn't give up on my dream of becoming an accountant. I spent my first three years at work, studying part-time to get my ACCA qualification. During my program, I also learned that qualifying as an accountant didn't necessarily mean I had to practice as an accountant. I could leverage my skills in risk management too.

Stories of people who transitioned their careers into other fields are abundant. These turned out to be the most incredible opportunities, or at least led to the most important life lesson.

My friend Busola Banjo graduated from the University of Nottingham with a degree in electrical and electronics engineering. She started her career as an electrical engineer in 2008. Seven years later, she decided to embark on an MBA at INSEAD to pivot her career into business. Following graduation, she got a job at Siemens Energy as a business development and program manager, blending her technical background as an engineer with her newer passion for business. It has been six years since that transition, and Busola is now head of a department.

Kanyinsola Oyeyinka is another example. I met her in 2006 during our Deutsche Bank, London internship program. At the time, she was an undergraduate medical sciences student at the University of Oxford.

After graduating, she spent about a year as a junior banker before returning to the medical field as a doctor for the following six years. Afterward, she became a healthcare investment adviser and then moved to Harvard Business School to study for a master's in public health.

You must not be so welded to the what, when, where, or how of your career that you forget about *who*.

As life happens, you will not always get what you want when you want it, but you can focus on who you are becoming. What skills would you like to learn, and what experience do you want to gain? What strengths do you want to hone? What perspectives do you want to explore? What causes do you want to add value to?

When you are clear on these, you'll become more open to what the universe offers you.

YOUR TURN!
1. Review the career goal areas mentioned in this chapter. Reflecting on the year ahead of you, set at least one SMARTER goal in each category.
2. For each goal you have set, do these three things:
   – Write out your commitments to action for each goal
   – Share these commitments with your chosen accountability partner
   – Set an alarm in your calendar to send a weekly progress report to that partner

CHAPTER SIX

Play to Your Strengths

"Accept yourself, your strengths, your weaknesses, your truths, and know what tools you have to fulfill your purpose."

—*Steve Maraboli*

****

Are you proud of yourself? You should be!

You have discovered your strengths, clarified what matters to you, set SMARTER goals, and are on your way to achieving them with an effective strategy. You are raring to go with all the new insights you have gained about yourself and ready to become more fulfilled, engaged, and productive in your work.

You may also be even more confused than you initially were. Perhaps you are wondering, *What now? What comes next? How do I put it all together?*

These questions were on Louise Johnson's mind too.

As an experienced lawyer working within a consultancy based in New York, Louise was handsomely paid to provide customized legal advice to clients on how they could restructure their business. Often, the client would engage her firm's services because they had a specific business goal, such as improving their tax efficiency, saving cost, reorganizing, or expanding to new geographies.

She loved that she could take ownership of a client's problem and provide a solution. Each engagement offered her the opportunity to learn more about the law and business and work with intelligent people in her firm and at her clients' firms. She enjoyed the company of her teammates so much that every Friday after they returned from their various assignments, they would meet at a local bar to have food, drinks, and a few laughs. Her colleagues had become great friends and a support system for her.

Despite all this, Louise often felt something was missing and she reached out to me for help. "I have been in this role for about six years. I like it, but some days I don't know what the point of all of this is," she told me. "I keep asking myself if I am on the right track or if there is something else I could spend my time on."

As I do with all my clients, we started with strengths. Louise engaged in her internal and external strengths discovery process with an open mind and curiosity. She wrote out her KASHI, took a psychometric test, and asked for feedback from her friends, colleagues, and close clients.

Her "aha" moment came when she took the CliftonStrengths assessment. Based on her answers, the test showed that Louise's top five signature themes were:

- Responsibility: she takes psychological ownership for anything she commits to
- Relator: she enjoys close relationships with others
- Learner: she has a great desire to learn and wants to improve herself continuously
- Restorative: she is good at figuring out what is wrong and resolving it
- Significance: she wants to make a significant impact in the world and influence her organization and the people around her

As Louise read her reports, she began to understand what was missing.

Over the past two years, Louise has been interested in social justice reform. This interest came when she went with some colleagues to volunteer in a legal aid clinic. There, she met with lawyers applying their legal skills to advocating for policy reform in healthcare, immigration, and the criminal justice system.

"For the first time in my career, I experienced how my work could serve people directly," Louise explained. "A big part of my current job is helping 'deep-pocket' organizations save money. So, if I do my job right, people could lose their jobs. I didn't realize how much this affected me subconsciously till now. I want my job to improve lives rather than destroy them."

Through her exploration, Louise clarified what mattered to her. While her role allowed her to take ownership of projects, work in high-performance teams, learn more about the law, and resolve client issues, it was missing an essential element. It didn't give her the sense of purpose and significance that her soul craved.

Having done the work to discover her strengths and clarify what mattered to her, her goal was to create better alignment in her day-to-day work. Since the volunteering experience, Louise started taking on legal work in her local community to keep the feeling alive, but that was no longer sufficient. She started looking for work in firms that had a practice focused on social justice reform cases or, at the very least, had a quota of cases dedicated to this type of work.

Since getting paid well was also crucial to her and her family who depended on her, Louise preferred to remain in the private sector where the pay is typically better. After almost a year of searching, networking, and interviewing, Louise secured her dream role at a law firm in Washington, DC, and made the switch.

Today, she is happier and more fulfilled in her career because she intentionally uses her strengths to accomplish the things that matter to her.

CRAFT YOUR CAREER

What is that career that intersects your passion, mission, vocation, and profession?

I know a word for this: a Japanese concept called ikigai (pronounced: *ee-key-guy*) that captures the answer to this question in the most beautiful way. It combines the terms *iki*, meaning "life," and *gai* meaning "reason," literally meaning your "reason for being" or the reason to get up in the morning. Ikigai provides a picture of a utopic future toward which you can begin crafting your career.

This philosophy, popularly depicted by the Venn diagram created by author and thought leader Mark Winn, encourages adopters to find their ikigai at the intersection of four interconnecting elements:

1. That which you love
2. That which you are good at
3. That which you can get paid for
4. That which the world needs

If you can craft a career that adequately compensates you for solving world problems by doing what you are good at and love, you will have hit the sweet spot.

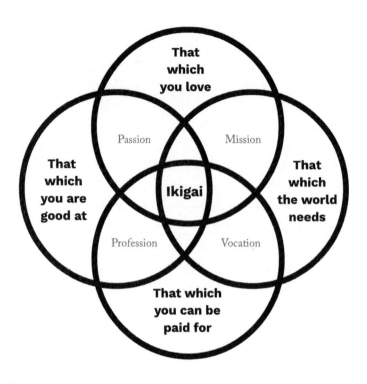

Source: Mark Winn, What is your Ikigai?

To explore what you are good at and what you love, go back to Chapters Two, Three, and Four, where we looked at how to discover your strengths and clarify what matters to you. These are the internal elements that anchor you.

On the other hand, what you can get paid for and what the world needs are external elements that evolve with technology, consumer needs, and time. With more innovation, the list of hot jobs or skill sets you can get paid for will continue to evolve.

Consider the impact of platforms, robotics, and Artificial Intelligence (AI) on many industries. Service robots in restaurants, automatic checkout stations at the grocery store, manufacturing service lines, self-driving cars, and customer service and marketing chatbots are some of the inventions that have made human jobs obsolete.

Therefore, consider the impact these changes will have on your career and earning capacity. Will people be willing to pay for your skills in ten to twenty years?

You need to ensure you are building skills in areas that will be relevant (ideally across industries) in the future so you can continue to be compensated for your time, energy, and value-add.

In their report *The Future of Jobs 2020*, the World Economic Forum highlighted a shift toward crosscutting skills like product marketing, digital marketing, software development, community engagement management, cloud computing, product management, data analytics, and diversity and inclusion management, among others. Consequently, jobs demanding these skills are expected to attract the highest pay in the next twenty years.

Interestingly, while each innovation provides a benefit, it often creates a new problem. For example, social media can bring us closer in a globalized market. Still, it has led to issues around data confidentiality, cyber-bullying, privacy, and low self-esteem. Consequently, you can dedicate your career to solving an infinite number of current and emerging challenges in our world, including reducing childbirth mortality, increasing equality in the allocation of social housing, helping people with their finances, protecting the environment, eliminating human sex trafficking, or improving the learning options for children with learning disabilities. You may have a lived experience with some of these problems and consequently have an intuitive desire to be part of the solution, or they could simply be problems you are close to or interested in.

Work toward having each of these four elements present in your career equation. "If you are lacking in one area, you are missing out on your life's potential. Not only that, you are missing out on your chance to live a long and happy life." (Winn, 2014)

Nevertheless, the point of ikigai is not to make you feel guilty. At various seasons of your career, you may prioritize some elements of your ikigai more than others. Acknowledging trade-offs will be necessary. For example, the opportunity cost of working for an NGO to solve a world problem may mean you have to sacrifice getting paid as much as you may like. Alternatively, you may need to work a corporate job with a high salary but have to sacrifice more of your time because of the job's demands.

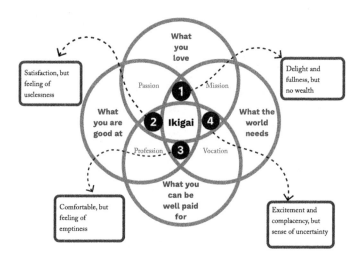

Source: Adaptation of Mark Winn's Ikigai Venn Diagram
created by Dreamstime

1. What you love + what you are good at + what the world needs - what you can be well paid for = Delight and fullness but no wealth. Your heart is full, but your wallet is empty.

2. What you love + what you are good at + what you can be well paid for - what the world needs = Satisfied but with a feeling of uselessness. You are not serving anyone else but yourself.

3. What you are good at + what the world needs + what you can be well paid for - what you love = Comfortable but with a sense of emptiness. You can afford a life, but you are unsure whether it is your life or someone else's.

4. What you can be well paid for + what you love + what the world needs - what you are good at = Excited and

complacent but with a sense of uncertainty. You are doing well but lack confidence because the skills necessary for excelling at the work are missing.

While not impossible, finding one job that intersects all elements of ikigai can be challenging. Your goal should be to incorporate these elements at various points of your evolving career to gain maximum satisfaction.

I advise creating your state of ikigai across a portfolio of activities. Take me, for example; I can earn a living as a risk manager doing what I am good at and enjoy alongside my work at viSHEbility, where I am helping to solve a world problem related to improving the outcomes for women in the marketplace. Don't get me wrong. Working in banking, I get to help solve many world problems when providing financing to some of the most innovative companies in the world. However, the impact feels less tangible than my grassroots work at viSHEbility.

CAPITALIZE ON YOUR STRENGTHS

Ikigai is excellent, but as I said, it implies a future occupational utopia that you need to walk and work toward every day. Ikigai is your macro view, but what micro-steps should you be taking?

Following a strengths review, reflecting on your current or prospective career to consider whether it is right for you is not unusual. You may confirm that you are exactly where you are supposed to be, or you may realize that you are in the wrong role and need to consider alternatives. This is often the case because, according to Gallup, only four in ten employees believe they are in jobs where they get to do what they do best daily.

In moving toward her ikigai, Louise Johnson made some significant changes—a new job, client focus, and location—but repositioning doesn't necessarily mean drastic changes or bold moves. "Most jobs have degrees of freedom . . . the trick is operating within the fixed constraints of your job to redesign work at the margins, allowing you to better play to your strengths" (Morgan Roberts et al., 2005). More often than not, making small changes in how you work, who you work with, and what you work on can tremendously change the quality of your experience in your job.

The **SPIKE framework** offers you five steps to apply to ensure that you are intentionally crafting a career that capitalizes on your strengths.

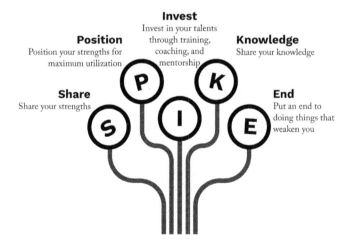

Invest
Invest in your talents through training, coaching, and mentorship

Position
Position your strengths for maximum utilization

Knowledge
Share your knowledge

Share
Share your strengths

End
Put an end to doing things that weaken you

SHARE

Share with others the insights you are gaining about your strengths. Ask them for a reaction. If they agree, ask for specific examples of when they have personally observed you operating in that strength. If they disagree, ask why. Doing this will deepen your insights, keep your strengths at the forefront of your mind, and help you attract the right opportunities.

POSITION

According to Gallup, to turn your talents into strengths, you must identify them (name it), appreciate their unique value and contribution (claim it), and identify specific actions you can take to use them more deliberately (aim it).

Ask yourself: Along what career path do I feel my strengths would be most valued? What projects can I get involved in that will better utilize and showcase my strengths? You need to use your talents frequently so that they can be enhanced into strengths, openly observed, and rewarded.

INVEST

Invest in your talents through training, coaching, and mentorship. The best athletes train intensely, and musicians practice their instruments daily to ensure consistently high performance. It will help if you did the same. Also, consider what activities you can use outside of your primary role to develop your strengths further. For example, volunteering with a start-up organization can improve your strategic thinking, problem solving, and teamwork skills.

KNOWLEDGE

As author and coach Stephanie Obi's book title says, knowledge is the new gold. Sharing your knowledge is one of the fastest ways to build a reputation for your expertise. Do not underestimate what you know and how helpful your knowledge can be to others.

END

Put an end to doing things not firmly within your strength zone. Find someone who considers that activity a strength, and delegate those tasks to them. This frees you to do what you do best.

SPIKE IN PRACTICE

One of my mentees, Rebekah, came to me with a problem. She had worked for her company for twelve years and liked her colleagues and the culture. She was well regarded and a valuable member of her team. However, her role was half as a company secretary, which she enjoyed, and half as a business manager, which she did not like. She also found a dual role quite draining and hectic to balance. Consequently, she wanted to leave her company.

Using the SPIKE framework, I coached Rebekah through this problem.

- **Share:** She took the 16Personalities and Clifton-Strengths assessments, which helped her revisit her strengths and values. She shared the results with me as her coach, as well as two other mentors.

- **Position:** Rebekah spoke to her manager about repositioning her role to 100 percent company secretary. She initially assumed it was not an option available to her. If her manager said no, she planned to offer up her time and do more secretarial work in addition to her current role for a defined period. She hoped the more she was identified as a company secretary, the less she would be asked to divide her time between two roles.
- **Invest:** I asked her to explore what materials she could read and courses she could take to develop herself further as a company secretary.
- **Knowledge:** I asked her to seek out opportunities to share her knowledge, such as writing articles, updating her team on industry trends, hosting training sessions on how to run a board meeting, and any other thing that could help her demonstrate thought leadership, improve her visibility, and expand her network.
- **End:** Finally, I asked her to explore whether any of her colleagues had the opposite preference for which role she prioritized, and whether they were open to taking her 50 percent business manager allocation in exchange for their 50 percent company secretary allocation.

Result: It took about eight months to execute, but the plan worked! She made the best part of her job the entirety of her job.

YOUR TURN!

1. Reflect on the ikigai philosophy and answer these questions:
   - What do you love doing?

– What are you good at?
  – What can you get paid for?
  – What does the world need?

2. Pick one of your talents you feel is underutilized. Using the SPIKE framework, explore how you can make minor tweaks to utilize your strengths more.

PART 1

Summary: Capitalize on Strengths

HERE ARE SOME KEY TAKEAWAYS:

1. **Start with your natural talents.** Your strengths are your most significant area of opportunity because you start with what comes most naturally to you. When you apply your talents, they can become your greatest source of fulfillment. You become more confident, happy, energetic, and likely to achieve your goals.

2. **Invest in your talents.** You have the power to turn your talents into strengths by investing in them through knowledge, skill, and practice.

3. **Look inward to discover your strengths.** You can find your strengths in your KASHI: Knowledge, Attributes, Skills, History, and Interests.

4. **Do not ignore your feelings.** Pay attention to the activities that make you feel FINE: Fulfilled, Invested, Natural, and Energized. These indicate your strengths.

5. **Look outward to discover more strengths.** Take psychometric assessments and seek feedback from others to discover more strengths and validate your internal strengths assessment.

6. **Clarify what matters to you.** You are far more likely to work effectively and succeed if you visualize your intended outcomes and set targets that keep you on the right track toward that intention.

7. **Set goals to turn the invisible into the visible.** Set specific, motivational, accountable, realistic, time-bound, exciting, and relevant (SMARTER) career goals.

8. **Support your goals with an effective strategy.** Move from merely setting goals to achieving them by implementing an effective strategy that entails writing your goals downs, committing to taking action, and a system of accountability.

9. **Stay flexible.** Maintain an experimental mindset and a flexible disposition to your career-planning process. Sometimes you will not achieve your goal, but that should not deter you from planning.

10. **Ikigai.** If you can craft a career that adequately compensates you for solving world problems by doing what you are good at and love, you will have hit your sweet spot.

11. **Capitalize on your strengths.** To ensure that your strengths stand out and you are intentionally making

career choices with your strengths in mind, put them on a SPIKE: share your strengths, position your strengths, invest in your strengths, share your knowledge, and end weakening activities.

PART 2

CONTRIBUTE VALUE

Solve problems and you will always be in demand.

**Understand what is important to those you
serve and deliver those relevant results consistently and innovatively. No one can argue
with value.**

CHAPTER SEVEN
Define Value

"The value is always in the eye of the beholder. What is worthless to one person may be very important to someone else."

—*Peter Ackroyd*

****

Have you ever considered what compels you to purchase a product?

Whether you are looking at a computer, a piece of clothing, or an umbrella, your buying decision often boils down to your perception of the benefit you would gain from having access to the product. This is value: the purpose for which something exists.

You may not recognize it, but you, too, are a product whose value is determined by your ability to solve problems and drive relevant results for your employer.

Focus on the word *relevant.* I use it on purpose. You may take actions at work that produce a result, but if those results do not contribute to the overall strategy of the mothership or the identified objectives of your stakeholders, those results will be considered irrelevant and, consequently, invaluable.

Let's say your department's strategy for the next three years is to expand geographically by winning more international clients, but all you present at every meeting is a list of new regional clients. Although you are still adding to the client base, your activity could be irrelevant.

A few years ago, I decided to reimagine and revamp a checklist to be used in the review of legal documents. It took me about one month to complete the work, after which I drafted an elaborate email to my team about how this new process would improve their efficiency. I got a few "well done" emails from my colleagues but nothing from my boss.

A few days later, he brought the topic up for discussion in one of our regular meetings.

"Why did you think it was important to spend time on this right now?" he asked.

"Well, it was a problem for me, so I figured it was a problem for others too," I replied.

"Did you speak to any of your colleagues before you began?"

"No."

"Don't get me wrong, you did a good job, but there are many other pieces of work that you could have helped progress.

Next time, I suggest you discuss your plans with me so you don't invest in things that are not a priority for the team."

Wow! I was deflated. The work I did was good but wasn't solving a pressing need, in his opinion, and I could have applied myself elsewhere to drive more relevant results. I had not taken the time to understand what was essential to my key stakeholders. Consequently, what should have been praiseworthy work didn't make an impact.

The hard but necessary lesson I learned through that experience is that delivering value begins with defining value, and I do not determine this value. Instead, value is in the eye of the beholder.

Your employer wants to know: What are you doing for me, and how is your work moving the organization toward the direction it wants to go? If you want to be of value, you first need to identify your stakeholders and understand their desires, problems, and goals.

STAKEHOLDER MAPPING AND PRIORITIZATION

Stakeholders are organizations or individuals that, in simple words, have a stake in your performance. According to the Project Management Institute, stakeholders are individuals, groups, or organizations who may affect or be affected by your decisions, activities, or outcomes.

This implies that your list of stakeholders could be broad. For example, you can have stakeholders within your organization like your senior leaders, business partners, colleagues, or those you manage or lead. You can also have stakeholders outside your organization like your investors, customers, suppliers, regulators, the government, and the community where you operate.

It also implies that there could be conflict in how stakeholders perceive your performance because of the unique way it affects them. One example could be that your investors may want to increase their returns through cost savings, which may mean fewer jobs available for the community. Another could be that your client wants to execute a transaction, which may mean you breach a regulatory framework. Whatever action you take, one person will feel your performance is good, and another will feel it is terrible.

At this stage of your career, the conflicts could be smaller but no less acute, like managing multiple deliverables for different stakeholders. In my work, I often review four to seven credit proposals at a time for various clients originating from numerous business units. At this stage of my career, I am also working on or leading several projects related to technology enhancement, regulatory compliance, policies and procedures, portfolio management, recruitment, and people development. In the fast-paced environment that I work in, many of these have urgent timelines I need to manage, and working on one often means that the other will have to take a back seat.

This is why you taking the time to identify and prioritize your key stakeholders before you jump into performing is critical.

In her article titled "4 Types of Stakeholders in Project Management," project manager Elizabeth Harrin provides a useful framework to categorize your stakeholders as Users, Providers, Governance, and Influencers. This model can be adapted to brainstorming stakeholders in your career at every level—your project teams, department, company, and industry.

Categories of Stakeholders

Users

Those that use your work product. These include your clients, current and prospective customers, business partners, senior executives, patients, future recruits, your team, and the public. Who uses your work? Who does your work benefit?

Providers

Those whose work inputs into yours. These include your suppliers, project subordinates, colleagues in other teams, junior teammates, and administrative assistants. Who do you need to get your work done? Whose delivery, or lack thereof, can impact the pace and quality of your work?

Governance

Those who provide quality assurance, advice, and guidance. These include your management team, human resources, career sponsors, industry regulators, and shareholders. Who has the authority to hire and fire you? Who is responsible for managing you and allocating work to you? Who decides your compensation and progression?

Influencers

Those who are not beneficiaries of your work or have an influence on it yet they can influence those who do. These include bosses and contacts of your managers, human resources, and admin assistants. Who has a relationship with your "governance" and can influence their decisions? Who has the opportunity to share a view on your performance?

While some stakeholders may stay on the sidelines, others can make or break your career.

Identifying and prioritizing your key stakeholders will help you effectively develop strategies to manage them. You will know where to invest your time, and you will better understand who you need to communicate with when making decisions that impact the success of the business and your career.

Mendelow (1981) offers the Power/Interest grid as an effective way to rank your stakeholder's level of importance. As its name suggests, the grid assesses the priority of each stakeholder by taking into account their ability to apply power or influence strategy or resources and their level of interest in the related outcomes. Although created for use in the project management field, you can apply this framework in your career.

The quadrant where you place a stakeholder determines the strategy you should apply in dealing with them.

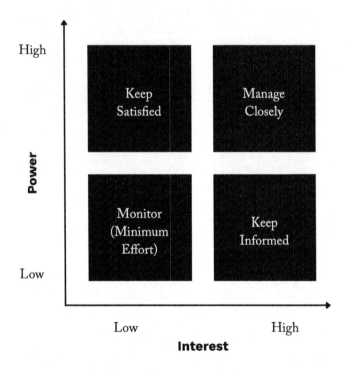

Source: Adapted from Mendelow, A.L. (1981). "Environmental Scanning— The Impact of the Stakeholder Concept," ICIS 1981 Proceedings, 20.

- **High Power, High Interest (Manage Closely):** These people directly influence your progression, pay, work allocation, and review. They can hire and fire you, and your performance directly impacts their outcomes and reputation. Consequently, you must engage people in this category and manage them closely. Your department's senior leaders, direct line managers, and project leaders potentially fall into this quadrant. The most crucial stakeholder in this quadrant is *you*. You have high power over your actions and are highly interested in your outcomes. Do not leave yourself off the page. Every other stakeholder is in addition to you, not instead of you.
- **High Power, Low Interest (Keep Satisfied):** These people have little interest in your performance, but they can influence your outcomes because of their relationship with those you work with or their position in the organization. Execute each engagement with them thoughtfully so you leave a good impression. Your C-Suite leaders like the CEO, CFO, and other influential people potentially fall into this quadrant.
- **Low Power, High Interest (Keep Informed):** These people are highly interested in your performance because they care about you or your work impacts them. However, they would typically have no formal power over your work allocation, progression, pay, or other matters. Keep them informed, as they often need to give their opinion on your performance and can also prove helpful in navigating challenging seasons. Your mentors, colleagues, and mid-level managers could potentially fall into this quadrant.

- **Low Power, Low Interest (Monitor):** These people do not have a direct interest in or control over your performance, so put little effort into managing them. However, you should monitor them if their level of power or interest changes. Your colleagues in other departments or organizations could fall into this quadrant.

Be careful not to apply a one-size-fits-all approach when segmenting broad stakeholder groups, since how you do so is highly circumstantial. For example, your direct line manager could have high interest but may have low power because of how decisions are made in your organization. In this case, you only need to keep them informed of your work. However, in a different organization, your manager could be a key decision-maker with high power and high interest, so you need to manage them closely.

Additionally, the position of a stakeholder can change as your role or their role evolves. For example, I had a manager called Matthew whom I "managed closely" because he had a high interest in my outcomes and high power over my affairs. Six months later, Matthew moved to lead a different team in the United States. Although he was no longer my manager (now low interest), he was a senior leadership team member (still high power). Consequently, my strategy changed from "manage closely" to "keep satisfied." I took on side projects to maintain my exposure to him so that when he was in rooms where my performance was being discussed, he was still in an excellent position to provide feedback on my work.

Similarly, you may be monitoring a senior leader in your field who is outside your organization because they have low power and low interest. If your company employs that person to lead your division, your strategy needs to change to "manage closely" or "keep satisfied" depending on their interest in your work and outcomes.

UNDERSTAND STAKEHOLDER
DESIRES, PROBLEMS, AND GOALS

Now that you have identified and have prioritized your stakeholders, you need to take the time to understand their problems, goals, and desires. Your job is to keep your high-priority stakeholders happy by championing and supporting the achievement of their objectives while also achieving yours.

As a primary stakeholder, your desires and goals are pivotal. What do you want to get out of your current role? What do you want to achieve in the short, medium, and long term? Review Chapter Four, where we looked at how you can clarify what matters to you, and Chapter Five, where we looked at how you can set goals and effective strategy.

Reaching your goal does not stop there. To succeed in any organization, you should align your goals with that of your stakeholders.

What are their most significant pain points? As it pertains to you and your work, what does bad, excellent, or outstanding look like to them? By what key metrics are they measuring such performance?

Businessman and TV personality Marcus Lemonis says that leaders in organizations are often focused on the "3 P's" of business: people, process, and product.

- Do we have the right people in the right roles, and are they productive?
- Do we have good processes in place for production, sales, billing, account, and customer relationship management?
- Do we have products and services that meet the evolving needs of our customers?

These problems are clamoring for a solution that could come from you.

Mojolaoluwa Aderemi-Makinde, who goes by Jola, is the regional head of brand and reputation at Google for sub-Saharan Africa. With a career spanning sixteen years in strategy, business development, sales, and marketing, Jola is adept at mapping out and understanding various stakeholder needs.

"Mapping your stakeholders is both an art and a science," she explains. "You can figure out your stakeholders by reading your job description and conversing with your managers, predecessors, and colleagues. You also need to be aware of the evolving influences in your organization, which you can only garner by observation and experience."

Once you do this, you'll find copious amounts of sources that can give you meaningful insight into what gaps exist in your industry, the company, your department, and your team.

In her current role, Jola drives small business development and entrepreneurship as part of the Grow with Google program. "It is important to immerse yourself in what is happening in the ecosystem around you; otherwise, you would lose the power of information," Jola says. "This is why I go to formal and informal industry events to capture information and stay on top."

One thing she highlighted as most illuminating was when she went into the market to interact with and understand her users and their pain points better. "Before we start drawing up spreadsheets and fancy decks with grandiose ideas of what we should do, we must confirm that what we are doing makes sense to the man on the street. My team and I need to recognize that we are in a bubble and not always a representation of the people that we serve. This is where getting external data and insights validates and even inspires the work that we do."

By staying engaged and curious, you can also identify the problems and priorities across the various stakeholder layers.

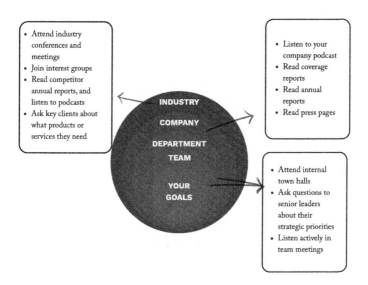

In their book *Power Questions*, Andrew Sobel and Jerold Panas recommend essential questions you can use to engage your senior leaders and business partners to understand their aspirations and goals. The point of these questions is to make the *im*plicit *ex*plicit, whether in group or one-on-one meetings.

1. What are the most critical initiatives for the organization over the next twelve months?
2. How do you think your strategy will change, given trends such as . . . ?
3. What are your priorities for the next twelve months, and how have they changed over time?
4. What significant projects or initiatives are you working on?
5. What are the most critical obstacles you are facing?
6. As you think about the future of the business, what are you most worried or excited about?
7. Are there any organizational or operational capabilities you will need to strengthen to support your future strategy?
8. How will your performance be evaluated at the end of the year?
9. Is there anything I can do to support you as you pursue your goals?

By doing these things and asking these questions, you start building a list of priorities from which you can select where you feel you can best contribute while keeping your portfolio of strengths and goals in mind.

Take the time to understand how personal objectives influence the prioritization of activities in your organization. You may have observed how organizational strategies and priorities change as leaders change. This is because organizations are a collection of people and ideas. A priority for the people becomes a priority for the organization.

"I have found that there is personal interest and strategic interest. Both are critical to understand because if something is important to the organization but not to your stakeholders, it is not going anywhere," Jola emphasizes. Essentially, what is valuable and relevant for the company is sometimes very different from what is valuable and relevant for your stakeholders.

Suppose a senior manager wants to retire on a high note. In that case, their focus for the year could be on a big project like building a new hospital or operating center, or creating a new development program that would serve as their legacy when they are no longer within the organization.

The best-case scenario is when your stakeholders' personal interests align with the organization's strategic direction. Unfortunately, this is often not the case, and you need to decide whose needs are most important.

Ultimately, the decision of who you choose to keep happy is a function of your ambition—the way and pace at which you want to grow, and your vision—where you want to go, what you want to get done, and who is likely to be in the way of you achieving those things.

YOUR TURN!

1. Using Elizabeth Harrin's framework, write down a list of your stakeholders in each category: users, providers, governance, and influencers.
2. Using Mendelow's Power/Interest grid, prioritize your stakeholders.
3. Spend time reflecting on how you will go about understanding the needs of the various stakeholders you have identified.

CHAPTER EIGHT
Deliver Value

"The right that you have to operate, to influence and to drive the things that you think are important comes from performance. If you're not performing, you have a lot less latitude to accomplish the things you want to accomplish."
—Mary Mosope Adeyemi

****

Imagine that you receive a beautifully wrapped package with all the best colors and trimmings. You open it and find out that it is empty. How unhappy are you?

Likewise, your stakeholders would be just as disappointed if you were all presentation without performance.

Delivering value is about providing a solution, driving results, and influencing outcomes through your performance.

Every form of progression in life depends on performance. In school, thresholds restrict who makes the cut and who does not. Mid-year exams and regular reviews are set up, so you know if you are in line with or deviating from performance expectations. Only those who exceed the performance threshold can move to the next grade. Exceptional students get opportunities for special programs and competitions that grant them access to better schools, scholarships, and many other perks.

On the other hand, those not meeting such thresholds are placed on a performance improvement plan involving school tutoring, increased parental involvement, and special assignments, all geared to improve their technical and critical thinking skills and their capacity for hard work.

Similarly, everything at work rides on the perception of your ability to help your organization achieve its objectives, now and in the future. Performance is the common denominator by which you and your peers are compared. If your performance is not good, nothing else matters.

Let me share the story of Tola, one of my clients. Tola started a new job at an investment company in the middle of the 2020 COVID-19 pandemic. Despite her excitement about the new role, her first three months proved to be more challenging than expected. She worked in the United Kingdom but reported to a manager in Asia. The distance made her feel she was at a disadvantage because her boss could not observe her daily activities or provide her with needed guidance. She lacked clarity on strategic goals, the key targets the team was working toward, and her manager's working style.

Her manager had already communicated a lack of satisfaction with her performance, which led Tola to consider leaving for another job. This was when she reached out to me to help her figure out how she could get back on track.

Working together, we did some stakeholder mapping and spent time crafting questions she could use to tease out what was important to them. After a few weeks of curious questioning and fact-finding, Tola realized what was most valuable for her management team and, unfortunately, where she fell short.

- Communication: They wanted to be kept up to date with projects and other deliverables. As Tola came from a job with more autonomy, doing this did not come naturally to her.
- Connecting the dots: Tola sat on several committees with different groups of attendees. Since she was a common person on each, the committee members expected her to help them connect the dots in the varied conversations. Until then, she had not even been aware that this was expected of her.
- Strategy: Tola's manager wanted her to support idea generation and not just execution. She had not seen this as part of her role until he mentioned it.

With this information in hand, Tola and I worked on some seemingly minor tweaks that would ensure she began meeting these stakeholder needs.

At the end of each day, Tola started emailing her manager with status updates on all her projects, satisfying his need for communication. With permission after each board meeting, Tola started sharing minutes of all meetings with members of all the committees she was on. She also became more intentional about highlighting where there may be conflicts in decisions made in each forum. I asked Tola to attend at least one industry seminar or conference every two weeks, after which she challenged herself to share one idea on how any of the "3 P's" (people, product, or process) could be elevated.

The result: Things turned around for her. She began meeting expectations. Her boss trusts her more and continues delegating even more responsibility to her.

PERFORMANCE = DELIVERING SOLUTIONS

After identifying your stakeholders, prioritizing them, and doing the work to understand their needs, the next step is delivering the relevant value.

However, delivering value through your performance doesn't occur by chance. Instead, it takes thought, planning, and execution. I suggest you apply six steps in order to deliver your best performance. These steps can happen over months, days, or hours, depending on the situation and the magnitude of the problem you are working to solve.

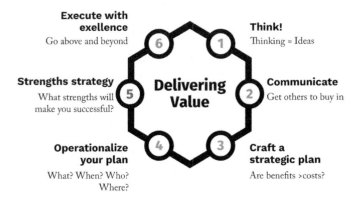

Delivering Value

1. **Think!** — Thinking = Ideas
2. **Communicate** — Get others to buy in
3. **Craft a strategic plan** — Are benefits >costs?
4. **Operationalize your plan** — What? When? Who? Where?
5. **Strengths strategy** — What strengths will make you successful?
6. **Execute with exellence** — Go above and beyond

STEP 1: THINK

You have done the hard work of gathering a list of pain points for your stakeholders. Create time to think through what you have found before jumping in. By making time to think, you will be able to:

- Understand the links between various issues and themes you have found
- Reflect on how your assumptions and beliefs have changed following your investigations
- Identify inconsistencies and errors in your reasoning
- Generate ideas that are supported by concrete arguments
- Determine the importance and priority with which pain points need to be addressed

Critical thinking will help you systematically identify, analyze, and solve problems rather than rely on intuition or instinct.

STEP 2: COMMUNICATE YOUR FINDINGS

Before investing more time, ensure you document the data, insights, and ideas you have collected and communicate your findings to key decision-makers. Doing this will:

- Inspire and mobilize people to support you
- Create space for curiosity and encourage others to ask questions, which will only make your execution process better
- Help you validate your ideas to make sure that your conclusions are, in fact, correct
- Secure early support to proceed from key stakeholders
- Fill you with energy and enthusiasm for the next steps in the process

STEP 3: CRAFT A STRATEGIC PLAN

An idea could be good, but it may not make strategic sense for your organization. Prepare a business case that compares the expected cost to the expected benefit of going ahead with a proposal. Some questions you must answer include:

- How much can we increase our earnings if we go in this direction?
- How much cost can we save if we go in this direction?
- What are the potential positive or negative impacts on our financial performance, market positioning,

and brand image if we responded in one way versus another?

- Is the timing right?

STEP 4: OPERATIONALIZE YOUR PLAN

A strategic plan is essential but not concrete enough to execute. You need to create an operational plan that defines the following:

- People: Who do you need to implement the plan?
- Product: What products feed into your program, and what product will be an outcome?
- Process: What processes need to change or be created to accommodate your project?
- Timelines: What are the milestones and deadlines that need to be set?
- Dependencies: Are there things that need to be sorted before your plan can go ahead?
- Roadblocks: What could potentially hinder you from executing successfully?

STEP 5: STRENGTHS STRATEGY

Examine how you can leverage your strengths to meet the current challenges and use that to create your delivery plan.

- Review the list of strengths you curated in Chapters Two and Three
- Consider what strategies and options you have for using your strengths to deliver value in a specific context

- Which strengths seem most helpful for this particular goal?
- What obstacles may get in the way of achieving this goal?

STEP 6: EXECUTE WITH EXCELLENCE

This is by far the most critical step. You need to be biased toward action and take responsibility for getting things done. Even when you haven't ironed out all the kinks, adopt a "progress over perfection" mindset, willing to begin the journey while being open to refining the plan as new information comes in.

Executing with excellence means going above and beyond to exceed stakeholder expectations by being resourceful and jumping over hurdles, operating without limits, and exceeding expectations.

BEING RESOURCEFUL AND JUMPING OVER HURDLES

This means not taking no for an answer even when challenged and demonstrating tenacity and drive to keep going until you finish.

Case in Point

When Uche Ezichi was an investment banking intern, he was assigned to prepare some analysis of the UK pension market. As he began his work, he spotted a vital research paper he wanted to read and reference from an external research source. Unfortunately, the latest version of the report was not due to be published till shortly after his deadline.

Rather than give up, Uche found contact information for the researchers and sent them an email asking for an advance copy of the report. They obliged and sent him a summary of the information containing all he needed. Of course, his bosses were impressed to see data from a report yet to be published in Uche's submission. It proved to them that he could be trusted to go beyond operating limits to get the job done.

OPERATING WITHOUT LIMITS

This means going beyond the remits of your functional role.

As a junior credit risk analyst, Wendy routinely read insight reports on various industries. After drawing her thoughtful conclusions, she shared the information with the head of the research desk even though she was in a different department. She wasn't doing it to get praise or strategically position herself; she wanted to be helpful. Her summaries caught the attention of the head of research, and he reached out to tell her that he found her summaries insightful. This gave her even more confidence to carry on sharing them. This regular interaction became the springboard for what became an incredibly strategic relationship for Wendy.

Today, Wendy is a partner at a global investment bank and credits the growth in her career to her mindset of operating without limits.

Something doesn't need to be strictly your job before you get involved. If something is broken, fix it. If you can make it happen, do so. Of course, you may have some concerns about overstepping. I suggest taking the initiative in the first instance, and depending on the response you receive, decide the best next step.

EXCEEDING EXPECTATIONS

This means achieving more than expected, like generating more revenue, lowering costs, or impacting more people than planned with the outcome of your work. It also means consistently delivering what you promised ahead of schedule.

Case in Point

Once, I was asked to lead a stream of an important regulatory compliance project. The project required the delivery of a new technology platform and the digitization of a critical process for documenting the approval of a subset of client requests.

As I progressed with my work, I realized that there were a few more use cases for the platform I was building beyond what was specified. Our regulators wanted a tool that was helpful for documentation, but by optimizing our solution, I could deliver one that could also be a one-stop shop for data capture, reporting, file storage, and approvals. The platform also enabled seamless connectivity with other tools in the firm, which materially increased the efficiency of the process.

When delivering the revised strategic plan, I told my internal stakeholders that the expected human time saved per year was one-and-a-half times more than initially estimated. I received unequivocal support from the operating committee to go ahead.

Based on the project timeline, I had eleven months to deliver the project. Still, I decided to at least show a minimum viable product as early as possible so I would have time to troubleshoot issues and iterate. With the help of a great team, I delivered that project five months earlier than planned. This also created the opportunity for the other project streams that depended on my work to begin earlier than expected, for which they were grateful. All the project leads were pleased and praised me for exceeding the plan in terms of scope and time.

When you deliver above and beyond, you move your stakeholders from satisfaction to delight.

INNOVATE YOUR PERFORMANCE

As market conditions and stakeholder needs evolve, the performance you deliver also evolves. I want to highlight four important strategies that are instrumental for you to innovate performance.

Leverage feedback
Proactively use feedback to fine-tune your performance

Up-skill
Identify and close your skill gaps

Take calculated risks and stretch yourself
Take on a "stretch assignment" that gets you out of your comfort zone

Diversify your perspective
Use new experiences to broaden your thinking

UP-SKILL: REFINE EXISTING KNOWLEDGE AND DEVELOP FUTURE SKILLS

To stay relevant, you must keep your knowledge and skills bank full. Business growth specialist Brain Tracy said, "Personal development is your springboard to personal excellence. Ongoing, continuous, non-stop personal development literally assures you that there is no limit to what you can accomplish."

As a lawyer, you must be aware of new cases, rulings, and statutes. If you are an architect, you need to stay updated with modern design and construction techniques. If you are a graphic designer, you must keep up with the latest design tools. Whatever field you are in, continue developing yourself so you can meet new and emerging challenges.

Read journals and articles, attend conferences, listen to thought leaders, and engage in discourse that keeps your mind agile and able to connect the dots.

Furthermore, in this rapidly advancing digital workplace, technology is replacing human tasks and changing the skills that organizations look for in their staff. According to PricewaterhouseCoopers (2021), 37 percent of the workforce worries about automation putting jobs at risk, and 74 percent is ready to learn new skills or retrain to remain employable.

Understand what competencies you need to demonstrate to give yourself and your stakeholders the confidence that you are ready to take up a new challenge, and then take the initiative to close any knowledge and skills gaps. Take the time to explore what online courses or programs are available to help you develop a specific competency you lack.

When bidding for promotion to portfolio manager, I knew this role required more presenting and influencing. I took a course on effective communication and joined Toastmasters to improve my communication skills. Also, when my role expanded to leading teams, I went on leadership development programs to enhance my ability to manage and lead projects and teams. After attending these programs, I intentionally practiced what I had learned in both instances, which increased my competence and confidence.

Nike Salami is a graphic designer working with an agency. She worked with corporate clients, but she had a keen interest in working with major film and music studios. She had not had the opportunity to move internally to the desk that manages such accounts. We started working together to build a portfolio of work that would be attractive to large studios. She took on freelance work and worked part-time with small producers. She also took an online filmmaking course to further refine her general graphic design skills for this niche area she wanted to go into.

A year later, she found out about a new role on that desk, applied for it, and was successful. The hiring manager told her, "Your interest in film and music was palpable during our interview. Your field experience will give us a competitive advantage with our clients." Up-skilling made the difference.

You could also consider going back into more structured academia. This is an approach that many well-known senior leaders take when they pursue an MBA or other executive programs to prepare for expanded business responsibilities or transitioning their careers.

Consider incorporating activities that develop lateral skills in your learning journey as well. These are typically underrated but effective in developing "out of the box" thinking. For example, creative arts can build your creativity, cognitive function, and coordination. Singing classes can improve your intonation, presentation, and ability to work collaboratively with others.

As a member of my church choir, I recognize that my memory, coordination, and confidence at work grew as I sang more at church. If I could sing to five hundred people in church on a Sunday, surely I could present a topic to a room of five people for ten minutes.

When all the learning is done, ensure you incorporate practice to continue sharpening the skills you are learning. Ultimately, you can only get better at something by doing more of it. Retain the posture of a student rather than the master. You can always get better if you remain teachable.

DIVERSIFY YOUR PERSPECTIVE

One thing that stands out to me with the executives I have worked and spoken with is the diversity of their perspectives formed through actively seeking new experiences. This could be from holding various functional roles in the same company or working with different companies, in different geographies, or across varied industries, all of which add to their diversity of thought and the richness of their perspectives.

Mojolaoluwa Aderemi-Makinde, whom I introduced in Chapter Seven, has had an intentionally diverse career. She studied computer science at university and started her career in an engineering firm before foraying into strategy consulting. "My background in computer science ensured that I was not afraid of technology," she says, "but I was interested in building my skills in business and strategy."

She went to work for Silverbird Group, a leading media company. Before long, Jola was promoted to lead the strategy unit working with entrepreneurs in a start-up environment.

A few years later, Jola made a difficult and seemingly irrational decision to leave Silverbird Group to take up a role as a junior strategy consultant at Accenture, a global consultancy firm. "I felt I was hitting the top of my career too fast. I had a huge platform and a wide array of responsibilities, but I did not feel I had a solid foundation. I had my fancy office, official car and all the perks, but I gave that up because I wanted to learn and build my base."

While at Accenture, Jola had the opportunity to work with clients across many industries and gained the technical foundation she felt she lacked. After about four years, Jola chose to leave Accenture. "I wanted to work across different product areas leading partnerships and programs," she says.

Jola joined Google as a business development manager. After a few years, she made a strategic career move to the sales department despite not having a sales background. "I had worked for Google for a few years and done a lot within the organization, but I didn't know about the cash cow of Google, which was digital advertising," she explains. "I didn't see myself as a salesperson, but I knew I had the ability to think critically, strategize, build partnerships and relationships. I went in with my strengths and accepted that the way I would achieve my quota would be different to other people's way."

Now a brand and reputation executive, Jola has brought together all the threads of her past experiences to deliver programs around education, digital skills, women empowerment, and training for small and medium businesses.

Don't be satisfied with doing the same thing day after day. Seek to do things you haven't done before. Move from operations to product development to sales to business development to compliance to customer management.

As long as you can connect your work to your strengths (your KASHI), every new experience will add color and richness to your perspectives and your CV.

TAKE CALCULATED RISKS AND STRETCH YOURSELF

The other lesson I hope you gleaned from Jola's story is how she took calculated risks that prioritized her learning and growth. At each stage, Jola assessed her goals and intentionally sought career opportunities to help her close her skills gaps and broaden her perspectives.

Notice my intentional use of the word *calculated* risk. Risk is the potential for a specific action not to yield its desired objective. For example, investing in the stock markets bears the risk of monetary loss. However, when risk is calculated, the probability of loss and your capacity to absorb it has been thoroughly considered. For example, when you study the company you want to invest in and review your financial situation to confirm that the loss you could bear will not be damaging, your investing action is a calculated risk.

Similarly, when making decisions in your career, the pros and cons have to be weighed. Taking risks is not a bad thing. As it is popularly said, "no risk, no reward." However, if you want to make a career move or take on a new opportunity but do not consider your probability for success given your strengths, then it's not a smart, calculated risk.

Stretch assignments are often a fantastic opportunity to take calculated risks. They are assignments beyond your current capabilities but extremely important to the organization, such as leading an important project, creating a new procedure, stepping into a new role, or moving to a new department to fill a gap.

They take you out of your comfort zone, demonstrate your capabilities, build your credibility, grow your skills, and strengthen your relationships with your stakeholders. They are often career-defining, but they come with risks you need to weigh against the benefits.

Whether you're being asked to take on the stretch assignment or you're putting yourself forward for one, executive coach May Busch offers three questions to ask yourself before taking on a stretch assignment:

1. Is it essential to the organization?
2. Is it right for me?
3. Can I stack the odds in my favor?

Not every opportunity is created equal. You have to choose well.

LEVERAGE FEEDBACK

In my career, I have received feedback on the quality of my work product, communication and presentation style, leadership presence, punctuality, visibility, dress, and so much more. Sometimes this feedback is about how well I am doing; other times, it serves as a nudge to develop in those areas.

In the workplace, proactively seeking feedback will help you fine-tune your performance to deliver value most effectively. However, many people are frightened of feedback, so the first step to leveraging feedback is evolving your mindset around it.

Unlike in school where you get grades that indicate a pass or fail, feedback is not judgment. Instead, feedback is guidance on what direction you may need to go or clarification on what needs improvement.

In their book *Power Questions*, Andrew Sobel and Jerold Panas recommend essential questions you can use to collect feedback from your stakeholders like your business partners, teammates, and customers:

- Do you feel I am working on the most central and critical issues for you?
- How can I do a better job of helping you meet your objectives?
- Am I doing an adequate job at linking our work to your key priorities?

- What have I done that has been most helpful to you?
- How could I make doing business with me easier?
- Are there aspects of your business you think I should understand better?
- Are there any other issues I should be aware of or thinking about for you?

Remember that the feedback process is just as uncomfortable for the giver as it is for the recipient because they usually don't want to hurt your feelings. Consider it a gift when others are vulnerable enough to share their thoughts.

Feedback is not merely about correction but also about collaboration. It allows other people to participate in your growth journey by giving you the benefit of their perspective.

PERFORMANCE REVIEWS

Periodic performance reviews with your manager are a pivotal part of receiving feedback to improve your performance. A performance plan discussed at crucial inflection points in your career is vital for continued career success. This plan must represent your agreement between you and your manager on what success looks like.

If your organization does not have a formal performance appraisal process, prepare your own. Think through your firm, department, and team goals, then link your job duties to these measurements.

When this is done, schedule an appointment with your manager to agree on what constitutes outstanding performance.

Revise your plan if needed and resubmit. Set up a periodic review with your manager so you have a checkpoint to gauge if things are going well or if you need to course correct. These meetings are critical in setting expectations and gaining support.

What should you be planning to discuss in these meetings?

1. **Communicate your specific value-added:** Be ready for the "How do you think the year went for you?" question. How did you contribute to the team, department, and firm goals? Talk in terms of numerical value. Write this out and send this in ahead of the meeting so there is a reference point. If you are working on a stretch project, provide an update on your progress.
2. **Your reflections:** Reflect on what could have gone better. What did you learn about the job, company, and yourself in the last few months? This is also an opportunity to raise any personal issues that could have impacted your performance. Don't make this a pity party. Stay facts-based and mention what you are doing to sort out the issues.
3. **Feedback discussion:** Consider collated feedback from your business partners and managers. Pay attention to this because perception is reality. It doesn't matter if you think you are doing a good job. What matters is if your managers think you are doing a good job. Use this opportunity to get a feel for relative performance as well. The point is not to compete, but the fact is that there is always a ranking process going on.
4. **Share your goals:** Share your plans and hopes for the future. How do you want to grow in the organization?

This is the time to be specific! Some examples of things you can share are:

- I would like to be considered for promotion.
- I would like to expand my network; please introduce me to XYZ person.
- I would like to work on a cross-geographical project this year.
- I would like to learn about a new product or cover a new industry.
- I intend on taking six months off or switching to part-time.

5. **Ask for what you need:** This is where you get your managers to commit to supporting you and your goals, such as:

- additional resources for a project you are working on
- reallocating more high-value clients or projects
- asking for sponsorship for the next promotion
- asking for a recommendation
- asking for the opportunity to run something on your own or lead a presentation
- asking to be sponsored for training

6. **Ask tactical Questions**: If you ask good questions, you get great answers. These are some questions to consider:

- What does success look like for me in the next six to twelve months?
- What can I specifically take off your plate that would be of most value to you?
- What do you require of me that I have yet to deliver?
- Are there any soft or technical skills you want me to improve?
- Are there relationships you want me to invest in over the next six to twelve months?

- Where do you see me being most effective and having the most impact in the next six to twelve months?
- If I wanted to exceed your expectations for me in my following performance review, what would I need to do between now and then?

Differentiate between constructive and destructive feedback so that you can respond appropriately.

Constructive feedback instills confidence in you while gently telling you what you could do to perform even better in the future. Solid evidence and well-thought-out recommendations usually support this kind of feedback.

As I became more senior, I got feedback from my manager that I needed to tailor my email messages to my audience. After asking clarifying questions, he showed me examples of my emails and helped me deconstruct how I could have worded them differently for maximum impact. His point was that I needed to understand my audience better and tailor my message to what each person cares to know.

For example, an email to a managing director should typically be brief and hit on the key points first because they don't have much time. On the other hand, if I was communicating with an associate or VP, they may want more details.

I left the meeting with much clarity and gratitude for the helpful tips he shared. Following this, I started spending a few minutes ahead of a meeting redrafting my message to suit the intended audience. I shared the first few with my manager for review, and once I felt more confident, I didn't need to do that anymore. It took time, but my emails were more effective.

On the other hand, **destructive feedback** is a tool used to hurt people's feelings. This feedback is hardly ever backed by evidence to validate the assessment, and you leave the conversation feeling defeated without necessarily knowing what you have done wrong or how you could do better in the future.

I have been in situations where I have vehemently rejected feedback because I felt it was laced with bias. I once challenged getting a "meets expectations" rating when I knew that my performance during the year was in line with an "exceeds expectations" rating. Rather than lay out the evidence, my manager suggested that I may have received a lower rating because of the way I dressed.

I was appalled by the comment, but I knew well enough that it was not valid. I have always dressed professionally, neatly, and respectably at work. I was commended regularly by other colleagues for how well I put myself together, so I knew there was enough evidence to refute her statement. This was a manager I knew didn't like me, and the comment was their way of being spiteful. I left the room feeling upset and escalated the issue to human resources.

This is why the message that "self-awareness is the key to self-mastery" is essential. If I didn't know myself, I would have begun running around trying to fix what was not broken.

When you receive feedback, you must sit with it and consider its root. Ask clarifying questions like, "Can you give me an example of what you just stated?" Ask others for their opinion if you are struggling with it.

Remember that feedback on areas to develop often targets blind spots, so it may initially be challenging to accept. But if there is sufficient evidence of its truth, you need to own it and take steps to remedy it. Take the time you need to understand your feedback and take action. You will never bypass a lesson you are meant to learn, so the quicker you learn it, the better.

YOUR TURN!
1. Select a problem or pain point you have identified in Chapter Seven.
2. Using the six steps of delivering value, plan how you will address it.

CHAPTER NINE

Mind Your Manners

"The ABCs are attitude, behavior, and communication skills."
—*Gerald Chertavian*

****

Have you ever had a bad experience with a company that made you stop buying from them?

I have.

A friend and I went to a five-star restaurant for a lovely steak dinner. After three hours of a perfect culinary experience, we paid for our meal, tipped the waiter for his excellent service, and left.

We had just walked out of the restaurant when we heard a loud, "Excuse me," from behind. We turned around and saw the bartender from the restaurant calling out in our direction. Knowing he had our attention, he shouted, "Have you paid?"

I looked around in horror and embarrassment as passers-by stared at us. *How rude,* I thought. *Even if he felt we had not paid, he could have handled that more discreetly.*

We walked back to the restaurant to show our receipt. Once the bartender confirmed that we had paid, he walked away with no apology.

I was so angry! I requested to see a manager, laid a complaint, and refused to leave the restaurant till the bartender was sent home. I was personally triggered; I knew he had racially profiled us as two Black people who didn't pay the food bill.

As we left, I promised myself I would never return to that restaurant again. I also shared my experience on social media, tagging the company.

How could we have such an experience at an acclaimed restaurant? How could someone's lousy behavior ruin such a wonderful evening?

This can also happen at work if you allow bad behavior to derail your good performance.

Your performance output can objectively judge value. Did you produce the results required of you? Did you deliver within the specified deadline and to the expected quality? Your performance output, after all, is about *what* you delivered.

However, value is also determined by how you behave and how your presence impacts others positively or negatively. Have you ever worked with someone to deliver a fantastic piece of work only to vow that you would never work with them again? Although they did a good job, something about their working style left a bad taste in your mouth.

These more subjective factors are about *how* you deliver the *what*. Do you pay attention to detail and produce error-free work? Do you work well with others? Do you add to or detract from a positive and collaborative work environment? Do you abide by public laws as well as internal policies and procedures?

In 2021, UK Health Secretary Matt Hancock was caught on camera engaging in sexual activity with his aide in his office. Later revealed was the confession that he hired her into that role so that he would be close to her. While there are no laws governing infidelity, the moral impetus for a man in his position was grave. He had performed well during his time in office, but his bad behavior has now tarnished his reputation and he was fired from his job. He will forever be the MP who hired his girlfriend and carried on an affair while holding the office his constituents voted him into.

In 2020, Amy Cooper, a white woman walking her dog, falsely accused Christian Cooper—a Black male birdwatcher she had never met before—of threatening her in Central Park. Amy had unleashed her dog in the Ramble, an area of the park where leashing is required. Christian had requested that Amy keep her dog on a leash, which was in line with the posted rules. Amy refused. She then said to Christian, "I'm calling the cops. I'm going to tell them an African American man is threatening my life." She placed the call to the police.

Luckily, Christian captured the encounter on camera, proving that she lied about the incident and weaponized her race and privilege as a white woman in a country where bias exists against Black men. After the story hit social media and news headlines, Amy's actions were widely criticized, and her employers fired her immediately. This is a cautionary tale that even when your poor conduct is observed outside of the workplace, it can lead to adverse consequences professionally.

Rules and codes of conduct are essential as they govern and control acceptable behavior in different environments. They are in place to respect and protect time, people, and processes and ensure that lack of compliance bears consequences. Ultimately, your behavior creates an image in people's minds about who you are and not just what you do. People hire and support those they like, and likability has its root in acceptable behavior!

These rules and customs are often referred to as etiquette, of which there are two kinds.

1. **Etiquette that is visible or documented** in your employment contacts, policies and procedure documents, signposts around the workplace, and even in your job description when you applied for the job.
2. **Etiquette that is invisible or unspoken** yet silently observable. "This is the way things are done around here" as reflected in practices such as dress code, working hours, tolerance for flexible working, styles of information sharing, decision-making, and learning.

Universal agreement about standard work etiquette doesn't exist, so it varies from one company to another, one country to another, and even one department or team to another. Therefore, paying attention to those visible and invisible rules and customs as you transition in your career is essential.

I once started a new job on the same day the company announced the adoption of an official dress-down culture across the firm. I was very excited about this, and I welcomed the prospect of wearing jeans and trainers to work every day like my friends working at Google, Meta, and other technology companies.

Over the following weeks, I played it safe and alternated wearing my formal and casual outfits. I observed some colleagues dress casually one day but revert to formal wear the next day. I also saw that my boss didn't wear casual outfits except on Fridays. This made it awkward when I attended meetings with him while I was wearing jeans. Ultimately, I decided that despite the allowance of a casual dress code, I would retain a semi-formal one since it appeared that was what my team stuck to.

On the other hand, the engineering team fully adopted the dress-down culture. I saw them often in the cafeteria during lunch and when I went to their floor in the building. From the senior to the junior, it seemed everyone was on board. What appeared to be acceptable custom was not the same in my department.

Through observation and asking questions, you can identify the unspoken rules in your workplace.

WORKPLACE ETIQUETTE BLIND SPOTS

Let's explore nine areas of workplace etiquette that are usually blind spots for many people. Failure to observe proper etiquette in these areas could negatively affect people's perception of you in the workplace.

ORGANIZATIONAL ETIQUETTE

These are the rules and customs to guide you in abiding by laws, adopting the organization's culture and values, and meeting behavioral expectations deemed foundational for a working environment to function correctly.

- Abide by all applicable internal and external laws, policies, and procedures.
- Be a good corporate citizen that seeks to understand business priorities and participates in addressing issues.
- Represent and reflect organizational culture and values as long as they are not in conflict with your values.
- Be punctual at work and in meetings.
- Demonstrate intellectual curiosity by asking questions and challenging the status quo.
- Adopt a problem-solving mindset that contributes to idea generation.
- Be diligent in carrying out your responsibilities.
- Be a team player by working constructively with your colleagues and offering coaching, mentorship, and sponsorship at all levels.
- Be respectful to everyone you work with.

- Do not speak against management and senior leadership except when giving constructive feedback.

Case in Point

One of BoA's well-publicized values is Deliver Together, which they explain on their website: "We believe everything we do for our clients, teammates, and the communities we serve is built on a solid business foundation that delivers for shareholders."

While I was at the firm, I saw this lived out practically in how business units collaborated to deliver solutions to clients. If one business unit cannot find a solution that works for a client, they are expected to bring in another business unit to pitch an alternative solution. Behavior in line with this ethos was celebrated while acting to the contrary was heavily frowned upon.

COMMUNICATION ETIQUETTE

These are the rules and customs having to do with the types of conversations you have in the workplace and how you generally communicate with others, physically or digitally.

According to Mehrabian's communication model, only 7 percent of any message is conveyed through the words we choose. The other 93 percent is found in subtle clues like our tone of voice and body language. Essentially, communication comprises more than just the words we use. Our facial expressions, body language, and tone of voice all play a role in how we are understood.

- Be mindful of how your body language, facial expressions, tone, pitch, and pace of your voice influence the message you are communicating.
- Master your emotions. This way, you can respond rather than react in difficult situations. Take the time to think before you speak, especially when angry. This is the best way you ensure that you remain composed.
- Listen actively. A huge part of communicating is listening. Sadly, as author and leadership coach Stephen Covey once said, "The biggest communication problem is we do not listen to understand. We listen to reply." Refrain from cutting others off mid-sentence and give them the space to complete their thought.
- Know your audience. Whether through an email or live conversation, tailoring your discussion to the needs of your audience is efficient and effective. Give more when more is required and less when less is required.
- Be mindful of sensitive conversations such as those on religious beliefs, political affiliations, and individual lifestyle preferences. While you should not compromise your stance, unsolicited opinions on these topics could result in unnecessary disagreements in the workplace.
- Do not be rude. It's okay to disagree, but you should do so respectfully. Avoid the use of profanity in the workplace as it is rarely well-received.
- Avoid jokes that any group could consider lewd and offensive.
- Avoid office gossip. Before you engage in it, stop to ask yourself: "Is what I'm saying true? Is it kind? Is it fair? Can it be repeated with my name on it?"

What you communicate is not only about what you say, but how you say it.

Case in Point

While on a video call with our manager, my colleague John had an outburst in response to something that was said. Even though he had a justifiable reason to be upset, his reaction was unprofessional. That moment stopped the meeting. Everyone left the session feeling awkward, like we had just witnessed a fight. John's behavior made him seem unapproachable, and the rest of the team became wary of him. As these things go, it didn't take long before the story of the incident spread around the department and poisoned his reputation.

However upset he was, if John had paused for a moment to breathe, he would have responded better than how he reacted in the moment. He could have pulled the other person aside to communicate his displeasure privately rather than publicly. That way, they would have been able to resolve their conflict, and their conversation would not have spread to the rest of the department.

EMAIL ETIQUETTE

According to Lifewire (2020), approximately 63 percent of professionals prefers email for business communication. With the advancement of technology and the increase in remote work in the wake of the COVID-19 pandemic, email use will continue increasing.

The challenge with email is that you will not benefit from using all communication cues to convey your message. You are also at the mercy of the receiver's interpretation of your tone, language, and temperament when writing the email. Consequently, you must pay close attention to your conduct over email so your words will not to be misconstrued.

All guidance related to communication etiquette applies when emailing. Additionally, take note of the following:

- Make sure critical structural elements are present.
  - The subject line ought to be meaningful and relevant
    Ensure your emails are well-formatted, readable, and concise
  - Always spell-check and review your use of paragraphs and capitalization
  - Close your email appropriately (e.g., kind regards, yours sincerely, etc.)
  - If replying to an email, address the recipient by the name they signed out with. Don't reply to "Doug" as "Douglas" or vice versa
  - Email signatures (if used) should include accurate contact information
- Read twice, send once. Take the time to read your email before hitting the send button. Be careful of the tone of your email and stay respectful. Do not put in writing anything that can serve as damning evidence against you at a later date. Always think, "Will I regret sending this email if it is shared?"
- Avoid "reply all" if not necessary and be careful of large distribution groups.

- Respond to emails promptly or confirm when you will send a response.

Case in Point

Gautam, a banker I worked with a few years ago, sent an email response to a client's request for a proposal. The client replied a few days later saying they would not accept the bid. When Gautam probed the client for a reason, they said that the email they received had a few basic errors that left them feeling we were not paying attention to detail. That something so small and avoidable could cost us a deal was quite a blow to the firm, but it was such a teachable moment for me.

Errors are not just errors. They can pass on the message that you don't care about how you present yourself and your ideas. Of course, we are not perfect, and mistakes do happen, but by taking the time to read over emails (or get someone else to read over them) before sending, you can avoid basic errors that could be costly.

MEETING ETIQUETTE

According to an article in *Forbes*, "roughly fifty-five million meetings are happening daily, and at least half do not accomplish much." Also, according to the *Harvard Business Review*, 71 percent of senior managers say meetings are unproductive and inefficient.

Considering this data, thinking ahead about how to conduct yourself during a meeting will serve you well in the workplace and not contribute to that inefficiency and lack of productivity.

- Be effective. Is a meeting needed? Can it be an email?
- Be efficient. Can the meeting be shorter? Appointments are often set for thirty minutes or one hour by default. An eight-minute session is okay if it is sufficient for all parties to achieve what they want to, so don't feel attached to a long meeting time.
- Be punctual. Showing up late to scheduled meetings is rude and communicates that you don't value other people's time. Of course, there are times when the lateness cannot be helped, but do not make it a habit.
- Be prepared. Ahead of your meetings, make sure that you are prepared. Read the discussion materials if any, prepare some talking points, and prepare a stakeholder map so you are aware of those who care about the outcome of the meeting.
- Be engaged and participate. Have good posture, write notes, ask questions, and contribute your opinions and perspective. Do not be afraid to give constructive criticism or challenge during a meeting, but do it respectfully.
- Listen as much as you speak.
- Put your hand up. Volunteer to take on work that moves the meeting agenda forward.
- Be constructive in your disagreements—taking the position that everyone has a common goal of serving clients—and advance the agenda of the organization.
- Make sure you understand the next steps you should take after the meeting and take action as soon as possible.

Case in Point

Earlier in my career, I sat in meetings and doodled on my notepad, drawing shapes, patterns, and cartoons. I picked up the habit as a child to help improve my concentration. Unfortunately, while I understood what it was doing for me, I was unknowingly leaving others with the impression that I was not interested in the discussion.

My manager eventually called my attention to this during our catchups. I explained why I doodled, and in response, she suggested I find other ways to demonstrate that I was engaged, like looking up and nodding, asking clarifying questions, and contributing ideas. I took her advice. In addition, rather than doodling random things, I started doodling the critical ideas from meetings to take down my notes. This was a more fun and productive way of note-taking. With consistency, the negative perception changed as I showed my engagement differently.

VIRTUAL MEETING ETIQUETTE

In the wake of the hybrid working model accelerated by the COVID-19 pandemic, virtual meetings now have a permanent place in how we do business. Pay attention to your behavior in virtual meetings.

- Have a dedicated space that is clean, neat, and free from distractions.
- Avoid sitting in public or noisy places.
- Be careful about discussing sensitive work content when other people are around and inadvertently sharing confidential information.

- Try to make sure your background is professional. If it is not, use a virtual background.
- Have good lighting (natural or artificial).
- Invest in a good camera and mic so you look and sound your best.
- Use the mute function actively so that there are no distractions from you during the meeting.
- Keep your video on as much as possible, as this mimics being in an in-person meeting. You also come across as more engaged.

Case in Point

On a virtual deal review call, a client spent thirty minutes answering analysts' questions. He was asked a tricky question about which he wasn't sure but managed to give a half-convincing answer. Suddenly we heard, "These analysts are like a dog with a bone. I don't know what I just told them. It was probably all wrong."

Of course, we were not meant to hear that, but we did. A careless mistake ruined the client's reputation, and some of the banks represented on the call pulled out of the deal.

PERSONAL HYGIENE AND DRESSING ETIQUETTE

While dress code varies depending on which industry you work in, it's almost always crucial to be neat and well put together. Present yourself in a way that would best represent you in a professional atmosphere. Just as building quality can make or break a hotel, your attire at work and overall hygiene and appearance can make or break your brand.

- Maintain good personal hygiene. Keep every part of your body fresh and odor-free. This includes hair, ears, nose, mouth, skin, feet, and nails.
- Dress to suit the protocol and practicalities of your job. Your dressing should not be a hindrance to your work. For example, you should not wear dress shoes as a coach on a ballfield or high heels as an emergency nurse.
- Avoid anything that would distract from your content or portray an image of incompetence.
- Avoid dressing in a manner that could be considered indecent in the environment you are in.
- Sometimes, you may need to dress for the job you want to be doing or create the image you want. For example, suppose you are working on getting a promotion and observe that those at that level tend to dress more formally. In that case, you may want to do the same to prepare for that next stage and portray a more senior image to decision makers.

Case in Point

Tunde is an information technologist who took on contract jobs at large organizations. Despite good reviews of his work, he found that his contracts were not renewed beyond the initial term. After a few years of starting and stopping, one of his colleagues summoned the courage to tell him that people didn't want to work with him because he had terrible breath. Though a difficult thing to hear, Tunde called a few ex-colleagues to ask if that was the problem, and they unwillingly agreed.

Tunde went to see a dentist, where he was diagnosed with Halitosis caused by a gum disease left untreated. With the treatment, his situation got better. While this may seem unfair, it highlights how poor hygiene can make others uncomfortable and unable to work with you.

DINING ETIQUETTE

Often, you will have to eat at work or dine with others as part of your work. Do so with respect and consideration for others.

- Study and abide by table manners such as the appropriate order of seating, using the proper utensils, and not talking with your mouth full, among others.
- Keep communal spaces clean and tidy.
- Beware of eating pungent foods in shared spaces.
- Be aware of the culture of eating on or off the desk.
- Abide by the recycling protocols.

Case in Point

Tracey was a business development manager fundraising for a growing technology company. This work made her travel from the United States to South Korea to meet potential investors. Over a planned dinner, Tracey dished her meal from the sharing bowls and tucked in. She was starving after a long trip.

Unfortunately, she had missed the memo that it is customary for the oldest to eat first in Korea. From her looks, it was evident that she was not the most senior in the room. Thankfully, the translator was able to step in and apologize on her behalf and gave her a signal to stop. She didn't secure the investment she came for. To date, she doesn't know whether her pitch wasn't strong enough or whether she unwittingly insulted her hosts.

SOCIAL ETIQUETTE

Social events are a regular feature in many organizations. In these environments, stories are shared and friendships are formed away from the busy demands of the office. Nevertheless, as much as social time is an opportunity, it may also be a pothole if you do not handle yourself properly.

- Use social events as an opportunity to meet new people and reconnect with your existing network. Get to know your colleagues and allow them the chance to get to know you.
- You don't have to drink, but be careful with the alcohol if you do. Remember that this is still work!
- Be cautious of your conversations and beware of crossing boundaries and oversharing. Don't assume people won't use it against you.
- If you would cringe if you watched yourself back on camera, stop!

Case in Point

Mike attended the annual Christmas party at his law firm. He got so intoxicated at the party that he grabbed his colleague's wife inappropriately. Ben, his colleague, was infuriated and punched Mike. Too drunk to restrain himself, Mike punched back, and a full-blown brawl ensued.

People stepped in to separate them and walk them out. The next day, the incident had to be reported to employee relations, and after a few weeks of deliberation, Mike was fired and Ben was suspended. Both of them misbehaved and had to face the consequences.

SOCIAL MEDIA ETIQUETTE

Social media has blurred the lines of work and life even more. It has never been more important to watch what you post and repost. The internet never forgets, and the content you put out can shape people's perceptions of you, ultimately impacting your career and life.

- Be mindful of your language.
- Remember that liking, sharing, and reposting a post means affiliating with the message.
- Be careful of how your content impacts the reputation of your employer.
- Everything you post or are tagged in leaves a digital footprint that you may not be able to erase.

Case in Point

I remember a specific person who applied for a role at my firm. Our screeners did a simple Google search of his name and uncovered some lewd photos and a post he had written with some prejudiced views on LGBTQ rights. Given this information, we decided to cancel the interview because we felt that his personal views conflicted with our organizational values of being inclusive and making the workplace safe for all, regardless of their personal choices.

COURSE CORRECTION

You may be reading this having committed some of these blunders and feel there is no hope of recovering from these mistakes. Don't fret! You can repair the situation by acknowledging the error, apologizing where necessary, and taking steps to ensure you no longer repeat them.

You may also find it helpful to ask a couple of trusted people to keep watch and let you know if you fall back into bad habits again. Chapter Five discusses the importance of accountability in achieving your goals. It may take some time, but you can demonstrate that you now know better and are trying to do so through persistent action.

In some instances, correcting the error may be highly challenging, and you may have to face the consequences—such as dismissal, a derailed career, and even time in jail. Even here, recovering after you have received your punishment is still possible.

An excellent example of this is Kweku, a former trader at UBS. He was convicted of illegally trading away two billion dollars when he worked in London, United Kingdom. In 2012, he was charged with two counts of fraud and sentenced to seven years in prison. In 2015, he was released after serving half of his sentence and later deported from the United Kingdom in 2018 after failed appeals.

During the three years between his release and deportation, Kweku worked with students, academics, regulators, and multidisciplinary corporate institutions across the UK. He's also worked with the UK government—including the counter-terrorism unit of the UK Special Forces, the Bank of England, and, ironically, the UK Home Office—to help deliver valuable lessons on risk management, ethics, complexity, and failure from his experiences.

Now living in Ghana, Kweku is a staunch advocate for cultural and systemic change in the finance industry with a practical and academic focus on ethics, responsible leadership, and purposeful—rather than extractive—financial activity. While he may never be able to trade again, he has been able to secure other job roles and keep his career moving forward.

YOUR TURN!

1. Out of the nine explored areas, which have been your blind spots?
2. Rank them in order of perceived impact and select the top two.
3. Create a strategic plan that increases positive and reduces negative reinforcement actions.
4. Select one or two people you want to share this plan with so they can hold you accountable.

CHAPTER TEN

Deliver Together

"The truth is—no matter how 'self-made' you think you are, you are made by many who have invested in your life. . . . Be known as the person that is investing in others to build them up as well. It's your way of paying back the debt that others have invested in you."

—*Josh Hatcher*

****

Think of all the times you had to do things alone. From going shopping, seeing a movie, going on a road trip, strolling in a park, running a business, or applying for a job.

Now think of how much better that experience could be if you were accompanied by someone or a group of people who genuinely supported you?

We are not created to be alone. Whether we like it or not, we need people. While the nature in which friendships and career networks manifest in one's life is different, friendships and career networks both play a similar role in their respective areas. Good friends keep your social life blooming, and career networks help your career blossom.

You uncover immense value when you can activate and optimize the people around you to drive the results you want to deliver. This is a common thread in the stories of many high achievers. At pivotal points in their career, a person or group always provided advice and support or helped them achieve their goals.

In career circles, these people are popularly referred to as your networks. **Networks are a group of connections and relationships that are made and maintained with the intention of achieving a mutually beneficial purpose or goal.**

In today's ever-changing job market, your network is one of the most critical assets to any career, the sum of all personal and professional relationships that help create opportunities for your personal and professional growth. Your network consists of not only people who will help you land your next job but also those who will perform the tasks you cannot complete on your own.

Networks provide a support system for encouragement, advice, and accountability.

Dara Treasdar was in the third trimester of pregnancy with her second child when the opportunity of a lifetime presented itself. A role as Chief Marketing Officer at General Electric (GE) Business Innovations and GE Ventures had opened up. If successful in applying, this would be her first C-level position at any company, which was a big deal.

At first, she counted herself out of the interviewing process because she assumed the company would not consider someone so heavily pregnant for the job. That was until a trusted advisor asked her a fundamental question: "Dara, why are you opting out before anyone counted you in?" This question challenged Dara, and she decided to give herself a chance. Dara got the role!

Since then, she has held other C-suite roles and is currently the head of global marketing and communications at Peloton, the world's largest interactive fitness platform. Her success wouldn't have happened if she had not heeded the advice and encouragement she received.

We all need people in our lives who can call us to be the best version of ourselves. When we think we cannot, they know what to say or do to make us feel like we can fly. They help us see what is possible. For me, this person was my father for thirty-two years, until he passed away in 2019.

Thankfully, I have an army of amazing women and men from varied backgrounds, experiences, and ages who have filled this gap. Some of these relationships have grown with me since high school and university. Others are those that I have intentionally invested in because of the specific experience each person brings to the table for me. They are always ready to answer my questions, encourage me when I need a reboot, and drag me back when I am going astray.

Networks provide awareness of and a pathway to new opportunities.

Deborah Ajaja had worked for the same consulting firm for seven years and was looking for a new challenge. She mentioned this to her friend, Tobi. A few days later, Tobi connected Deborah to a senior leader at LinkedIn, whom she met a few years prior. That connection led to a new job for Deborah as the head of UK and Ireland go-to-market operations at LinkedIn Marketing Solutions. The role offered more money, better work-life balance, and improved career prospects.

According to HubSpot, 85 percent of jobs globally get filled through personal and professional connections. In fact, according to CNBC, 70 percent of jobs never get published publicly. Many organizations even offer bonuses to employees who refer their friends for roles, removing the need to post positions.

Digital networks are also taking this capability to the next level. Today, LinkedIn is the largest professional network on the internet, with 830 million members in more than two hundred countries and territories worldwide (LinkedIn, 2022). The network functions based on three degrees of separation, which allows you to see and share opportunities with those you are directly or indirectly connected with.

LinkedIn has been invaluable to me in gaining access to opportunities. I have been contacted by recruiters, invited to speak at events, and used it as a platform for my thought leadership on issues that matter to me. Frankly, the opportunities are endless.

Whenever you have a need or problem, remember that you are only one physical or virtual connection away from the solution.

Networks can provide credibility by putting the power of their brand behind us.

When the CEO of Walgreens Boots Alliance, Rosalind (Roz) Brewer, secured her first board seat, it happened at the recommendation of Wayne Sanders. Wayne, a white man, had been on the board of Molson Coors Brewing for years and had a mission to improve the board's diversity profile.

Wayne saw Roz in action when they both worked at Kimberly Clark where he was CEO and she held several management positions. While he knew she could do the job, he was also aware of the systemic biases that work against Black women like Roz. To achieve this, he willingly gave up his board seat on the condition that Roz was appointed as his replacement. "Wayne picked me up and put me in that seat. He saw something in me and kept saying, 'Don't worry, you'll learn it.' And I did. But I also learned it because I knew I had Wayne counting on me and expecting me to do well." Wayne staked his reputation so that the change he wanted to see would happen.

Throughout your career, many decisions will be made about your progression in rooms you are not in. Whether for a new job, a promotion, a business proposal, or a funding request, people in your network can provide the stamp of approval you need.

Imagine my surprise when I walked into a job interview and saw a former colleague on the interview panel. James and I had worked closely at a previous company, and although we did not stay in close contact, we had fond memories of working together.

James didn't take it easy on me during the interview, but as I left, I knew his support would be crucial to securing the role. As an old colleague, he knew me better than everyone else on the interview panel. He could vouch for my knowledge, experience, and style of operating, and he would be in the best position to address any objections. I was right! I got the job.

Networks provide access to people, ideas, and other resources that elevate our capacity to execute.

In 2021, Google and Alphabet employees who identify as Black hosted an informal learning session on angel investing. Employees organized it so anyone interested could learn about how start-up deals are structured and get ideas of businesses they may want to invest in together.

"Within two weeks, five attendees came together to turn that idea into reality. Then more raised their hands, asking how to participate. Fast forward, and the organization Black Angel Group (BAG) now features thirty-five Black leaders and operators inside of Alphabet, including from Google, GV, CapitalG, YouTube, and Gradient Ventures." (Tech Crunch, 2021)

These leaders invest their money and collective expertise—from product management to digital marketing to people operations—in founders who build ethical, high-growth technology companies. In the first year, they invested more than $500,000 in twelve companies, including Career Karma, Outlier, PayHippo, and FitGrid.

With less than 4 percent of venture partners and just 1 percent of angel investors identifying as Black, BAG is also creating a new generation of angel investors and economic opportunities for the Black community. Each individual may have had the idea and interest to invest in start-ups but may not have been successful. But by tapping into the network's power, they could pool their ideas, capabilities, and funding to do more than they could on their own.

I benefited from this in my work as a career strategist. I held my first group program for early career professionals in February 2021. The continuing success of that program results from the people I had around it. Eight out of twelve students in the first cohort were young women I met at events, taught, or worked with in the past. Six out of eleven students in the second cohort were referrals from the students in the first. To top it off, one of these students recommended me as a workshop host for a leading consulting firm, which opened up more opportunities with other companies.

My network has been critical in helping me connect to organizations and social circles that I wouldn't have had access to otherwise. Knowing how to activate your networks can transform your work and the results you generate. You can go much further much faster.

THE COLLABORATIVE MINDSET

According to LinkedIn, approximately 80 percent of professionals considers networking essential to career success. However, 38 percent of professionals has difficulty fostering strong networks despite their importance. Some are of the school of thought that networking is self-serving, in that people who network are only out to get something from others rather than give. Others attribute it to a lack of time, shyness, discomfort, or introversion.

Then there are those, like me, who don't grow our networks because we do not know how to. That was until I started understanding the power of collaboration.

I was always a strong individual contributor, but when I began working, I realized that I was missing half of the magic. When I opened myself to working with others, I saw how much stronger my work product could be. When I worked in a team, I observed how each person viewed a problem differently because of their background and experience. They also played to their strengths; one person was great with numbers, the other was great with words, someone was great with design, and another was great at presenting.

Working with others brought diverse thought and richness to our decision-making and execution. I learned to appreciate that this collective input improved my output. This is a collaborative mindset, one where you seek to work with diverse groups of people because you know the collective outcome is better than what you can deliver as an individual.

The collaborative mindset finds its root in:

- **Curiosity:** What could be missing, and what questions haven't I asked?
- **Openness:** How can my work be better, and what can others contribute to my thinking?

- **Reciprocity:** I know I have a lot to offer, so how can I add value to others?
- **Safe Connection:** How do I find safety in sharing my ideas and helping others with theirs?

When done right, collaboration can create a sense of community and sometimes even family. True collaboration places value on all interactions, and our networks are just a critical part of how we get things done and develop ourselves. Fostering this mindset can also help you overcome your aversion to forming networks.

THE KEY TYPES OF NETWORKS

When I started my career, I used to think networks were a single homogenous group of people who serve the same purpose. They were the people I could talk to and with whom I could ask questions, people I could get information and intel from, and people that could act as a sounding board for me. However, when I participated in a leadership development program in 2016, I learned that networks should be categorized so you can have more clarity in the relationships.

A few thought leaders have offered some helpful frameworks for this categorization. Executive leadership coach May Busch says that within your community of supporters, there are five special categories of people you need in a professional network:

- **Mentors** are those with more expertise and experience than you and are willing to give you advice. They're people you trust and whom you turn to for guidance.

- **Sponsors** are those within your organization or industry in a position of power willing to advocate for you and use their political capital to help you advance. That these people need to be more senior than you is a common misconception; that is not necessarily the case. The critical criterion for sponsorship is influence, not seniority. Someone younger or less experienced than you may find themselves in a position to advocate for you in spaces you are not in.
- **Peer coaches** are a small group of people going through similar challenges and can offer advice and guidance.
- **Connectors** are well-connected people who enjoy making introductions to people in their broad networks. They're hugely valuable, especially if you're an introvert, time-strapped, or both. Connectors can save you time and anxiety while helping you build relationships.
- **Raving fans** are loyalists who speak well of you wherever they are. They are happy to support you and boost your energy and confidence. They're also people who can help you build networks by making introductions or saying good things about you to key stakeholders.

In their *Harvard Business Review* article titled, "How Leaders Create and Use Networks," Herminia Ibarra and Mark Lee Hunter categorized networks into personal, operational, and strategic networks, as depicted below.

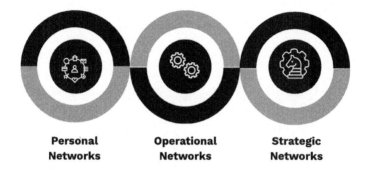

Personal Networks **Operational Networks** **Strategic Networks**

PERSONAL NETWORKS

These are your family, friends, and members of affinity groups you belong to. They are people whom you hang out with informally, and they can provide a safe space for you to get insight and advice and seek solutions.

The most important thing to these people is you coming out on top and being safe, healthy, and in the right place.

OPERATIONAL NETWORKS

These are people at work who have the knowledge and capacity to help you get your work done. To a large extent, the relationships in this category are prescribed by your job and organization structure.

The most important thing to these people is getting the work done. They want to ensure that there are no kinks in the hose as it pertains to completing the project, the task, or the transaction, and they partner with you to ensure that items on the to-do list are checked off.

STRATEGIC NETWORKS

These external and internal relationships help you understand what is happening beyond your current seat and expand your capacity to take on future challenges and priorities.

These relationships transcend organizational and functional boundaries. They are primarily concerned about the organization and how your growth will move the collective agenda forward. This is the most challenging network to form and the most important to career progression.

In the same leadership development program I participated in during 2016, I was given an exercise to write down the names of the people in my network and categorize them into each of these buckets. It immediately became apparent that I had more personal and operational relationships, which I had formed organically, and almost no strategic relationships.

I had friends to listen to my sob stories, party with me, and give me advice. I also had an army of assistants, analysts, technical specialists, and other business partners who helped me execute to a high standard for my clients daily.

The collaborative mindset I developed played a massive part in those two. Still, it didn't help me with the most critical category.

I lacked relationships with those who had the power to influence my progression within the firm, help me connect the dots, or provide sponsorship for my next opportunity. This revelation happened at a pivotal point in my career.

The second task was to identify those I wanted in my strategic bucket and devise a plan to grow these without neglecting my personal and operational networks. This was a real challenge, and to be honest, it still is. Strategic networks require intentionality and investment of time because they are more likely to be with people with whom we have less common ground and affinity.

As I pondered who I should include in my target list, I focused on five groups:

- People who influenced my pay and progression within my organization, like my manager and department heads.
- People whose work I found interesting and where I could see future career prospects.
- People who modeled attributes that I aspired to both in and out of my organization.
- People who were in my sub-industry outside of my organization.
- People who were passionate about the things that I cared about.

They reflected my ambition (how I wanted to grow) and my vision (where I wanted to go).

I then leveraged the people in my personal and operational networks to make introductions. I reached out directly by email to those who worked at my company. I used digital tools like LinkedIn to send connection requests. I attended events where I knew I might meet them and joined affinity networks and interest groups they belonged to.

In some cases, I went as far as to take interviews in the risk division of other companies to meet the senior people there. I was on a mission to increase my connections.

The journey held some pleasant surprises. In 2017, I signed up for a Vital Voices annual mentoring walk. This global initiative brings together mentors and mentees to walk in their communities, sharing challenges and solutions and forming supportive bonds that foster growth, confidence, and leadership. My goal was to meet other working women and also get a mentor.

During this event, I was paired up with Sylvana Caloni, a finance professional, leadership coach, and ex-president of the Women in Banking and Finance network. What started as an awkward three-hour walk with a woman I had only met that morning ended up being the most extraordinary meeting of minds. We had many common interests and passions, and I learned so much from her that day.

What I didn't expect, however, was that Sylvana was going to serve as a critical sponsor by nominating me for the Women in The City Rising Stars Award in 2017, which I won. That award has been the catalyst for many amazing things in my life and career. And it all started with intentionally focusing on building my network.

Every so often, I suggest you take the time to reflect on your networks and consider whether they fit your purpose. Are they a reflection of your ambition (how you want to grow) and your vision (where you want to go)?

THE QUALITIES OF A WINNING NETWORK

As you and your career evolve, reevaluate your networks and ensure they are structured to support your current and future goals. Your networks need to be:

- **Supportive:** Your network should be a group of people who are invested in your success and are present through all seasons.
- **Diverse:** Your network should include people who are different from you. It should have people of other races, genders, sexual orientations, socioeconomic backgrounds, religions, and professions. This will offer you a diversity of thinking and experiences for you to glean from.
- **Empowering:** Your network should help you advance, give you access to information and opportunities, and boost your confidence to take action in your career journey.
- **Evolving:** Your network should grow as you grow so you are not spending year upon year always seeking information and advice from the same people.

- **Mobile:** Your network should transcend distance—especially in this global marketplace—so your investment is never wasted.

THE SIX P'S OF MAKING SUCCESSFUL CONNECTIONS

Cultivating a personal and professional network is essential to your career success, and it begins by making connections with others.

You can meet people in various ways, including one-on-one meetings, virtual forums, networking events, affinity networks and interest groups, and introductions and referrals from others. Some of these approaches will work for you, while others will not. For instance, I've always been averse to large-scale networking events!

Earlier in my career, I was nervous about meeting people in this setting. I didn't particularly appreciate having conversations about random topics, trying to sound exciting, competing for airtime, navigating how to join or leave a conversation, and the etiquette of standing with a canapé in one hand and a drink in the other. I recall many events during which I grabbed a drink and quickly walked the room saying a few hellos before heading to the nearest bathroom to hide away if I didn't meet someone I knew or connected with immediately. I would pick up a book and read until the networking event was over. The memory still fills me with dread.

Nowadays, you can adapt networking to a method that works for you. In-person networking events remain among the most effective for connecting with like-minded people. However, the rise of digital platforms (such as LinkedIn and Instagram) and video conferencing (via Zoom and Teams) means you can also form connections virtually.

According to a study by Techjury in 2021, 40 percent of people say that they network more online than in person. LinkedIn also found that nearly two-thirds of professionals globally agree that regular online interaction with their professional network can lead to possible job opportunities.

However you choose to connect with others, consider the tips below to make your experience more enjoyable and effective.

- **Purpose:** A big myth is that you must attend every networking event, but the opposite is true. You only need to participate in a handful of events with a clear mission. Who do you want to meet? What would you like to learn? What do you want to gain out of attending this event? Being clear on your why will ensure you have a plan before getting to the event.
- **Prepare:** Take the time to research speakers and attendees. Prepare some tailored questions and even an elevator pitch; you will immediately come across as interested and engaged.
- **Participate:** Be willing to ask questions and share your thoughts and perspectives. Take every opportunity to tell people what you are doing as well. I remember an event at Google for Black founders. Tokunbo Koiki, the founder of Tokunbo's Kitchen, was in attendance. I had never met her, but when she stood up to ask her question, she delivered one of the most fantastic

elevator pitches I had ever heard. The room was impressed, and it showed. When it was time for the networking segment, other attendees flocked toward her to find out more about her business.

- **Provide:** Your disposition toward networking can vastly improve when you focus on the value you can add to your network rather than what you can get from them. What value can you immediately provide, and what can you do for others due to the relationships you already have? Always remember that networking is not just about connecting with people but also about "connecting people with people, people with ideas, and people with opportunities" (Jennae, 2013). Networking will start feeling more natural, authentic, and empowering when you approach it with this mindset.

- **Polite:** This goes without saying, but good manners go a long way. Dress appropriately, be on time, and be respectful in your communication.

- **Produce:** Follow up immediately after the event and do what you promised. There is a tiny window to deepen connections after an event, so make sure you take advantage of this quickly.

ACTIVATE YOUR NETWORK TO YIELD RESULTS

Bukola Adisa, founder and CEO of Career Masterclass, is a good friend and big sister to me. Two years before we met, I consistently heard her name from people who thought we should connect.

At the time, Bukola was a managing director in the Chief Controls Office at Barclays, a level of seniority that very few

Black women attain in the UK. She also led an organization focused on developing Black and ethnic minority professionals, a passion we had in common.

When I discovered she was hosting a training session on confidence at Deloitte, I knew it was the opportunity I was waiting for to make the connection. I went along and learned a lot. At the end of the event, I walked up to her and introduced myself. I told her all the things that inspired me about her and asked if she would like to get coffee in the coming weeks. She was open to it, and we exchanged phone numbers.

Two weeks later, she reached out to me to deliver a session at a conference she was hosting. As someone who always wants to lead with value, I didn't hesitate and agreed. Following that event, I invited her to be a guest on my talk show. Since then, we have fostered a tremendous active relationship.

I have regularly tapped her for advice and resources, met her family and friends, attended a concert with her, connected her to people, and we have been cheerleaders for one another. We took a well-intentioned connection and developed it into a relationship that serves us both.

Sadly, many professionals do not invest in their networks regularly and wait till they need something. According to LinkedIn, less than half of professionals (48 percent) keep in touch with their network when things are going well in their career (LinkedIn, 2017).

If you do not activate your networks, they will be useless to you. You need to ask and answer questions. You need to seek and provide advice. You need to offer and request help. You need to share and listen. All of these create the opportunity to extract value from and be valuable to others.

At times, I've wasted much time striving to get something done only to realize that someone around me could have helped if I had asked. In activating your network, remember that "if you don't ask, you will not get."

The **SECURE framework** below offers you essential tips to turn your connections into activated relationships.

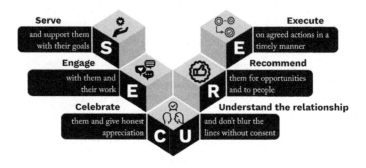

Serve

Nothing activates a relationship like service. Learn to lead with value by offering your strengths and resources to assist others with their goals. People often ask, "What if I have nothing to offer?" To that, I say this: everyone has something to offer.

Being of service means being helpful, which means different things to different people. Mundane activities like sharing relevant articles or extending an invite to an industry event can benefit others. You can also provide heavy-lifting help, such as volunteering with a network member's community or organization, being a speaker at an event they are running, proofreading their articles, or helping with social media. As long as it reduces their burden and frees up their time, they would appreciate it.

Engage

Regular contact is vital to keep a relationship active. Reach out to your network regularly, not just when you need something. Check in to find out how they are. Attend events they organize and extend an invite to them when you have something going on. Organize a virtual call to catch up on their progress on a project they are executing. Engage with their work and social media content (like, comment, share, and subscribe).

Also, seek their opinion on your work and offer yours when they ask. These actions will make them feel that they are a part of your journey and not just an observer. They will also keep your name on their minds.

Celebrate

You must give honest appreciation to your network for the value they provide to you.

If someone helps you secure a deal, take them out for lunch or dinner. If someone gives you advice that pays off, give them a gift. If someone produces fantastic work for you, write a recommendation on LinkedIn that provides credibility to their skills and impact. If someone invests time in you, send a thank you note.

Be someone that lavishes gratitude on others. No one likes a thankless job, and when someone openly celebrates you, it's difficult not to support them.

Understand the Relationship

You must understand whether the various relationships you have in your network are of a professional or personal nature. Managing mutual understanding of the relationship is less about how you activate your network and more about what to avoid if you don't want to *deactivate* it. Ensure that boundary lines are clearly stipulated at the start and only adjusted when mutual consent exists. Crossing the line can be very damaging to a relationship and ultimately to your brand.

What makes the relationship work or not work? If you want a good relationship with your boss, you need to know how they like to be approached and what kind of behavior makes them happy. Be open-minded about other people's needs and interests and avoid imposing your views on them. This will help build mutual trust between you and others, which is one of the most critical aspects of building stronger relationships.

Recommend

A tangible way of adding value to your network and keeping it activated is recommending people within for opportunities that would be valuable to them. Consider recommending them for jobs, visibility opportunities, business prospects, awards, PR features, and other opportunities. You can also recommend them as a resource to others. Doing this helps members of your network expand their network, influence, and impact. It also encourages them to return the favor.

Execute

If you want your relationships to continue growing positively, you must ensure you execute on agreed deliverables. If you say you will do something, do it. Additionally, if someone offers you advice, be intentional about following up with what you decide. You do not have to take their advice, but tell them what you've chosen to do and why. Let them know the results of your decision either way. This way, if they keep helping you, they will be more inclined to do so because they know how you received their last suggestion and how you did or did not experience the results. Results encourage both parties to keep the connection active.

INNER CIRCLE SUITABILITY CRITERIA

As we wrap up this chapter, I must emphasize that due care and caution should be applied when selecting those that will play a more meaningful role in your career and life. I call them your inner circle. They are the ones who know how your kitchen works, and whose advice influences the decisions you make. In making those choices, keep these factors in consideration:

Shared Values: Your inner circle should share the same core beliefs that guide behavior. If the pursuit of happiness is a core value for you, seeking advice from someone whose primary motivation is money over how happy their life is will be pointless.

Tanaka, a wealth manager, contacted me to mentor her. When I asked her why she thought I would be an excellent mentor to her, she said, "I have observed that your Christian faith guides your work, and that is important to me." Faith was a core value for her, and we were aligned. For you, it may be balance and flexibility, health and wellness, or helping others. What values are important to you, and in whom have you seen those values activated?

Trust and Care: Fill your inner circle with those you can trust with your goals, those who will do what is necessary to keep you from quitting, those who can act as your conscience when life gets in the way of your plans. They must have the time to ask you how things are going, and they want to be there to celebrate your wins with you because they genuinely care about you and the outcomes you are striving for.

Reputation and Evidence of Success: Your inner circle should have experience and proof of success in the area where you want guidance. Don't take business advice from someone who has never run a business. Don't take financial advice from someone whose finances are a mess, and do not take career advice from someone who has never had one before. Do your research, speak to other people they have mentored, and find evidence in their lives of the success you want to achieve for your own.

Role Modeling: Your inner circle should model behaviors you admire and want to develop. One of my colleagues, Ruben, is a role model to me because of his work ethic and outstanding communication skills. Whenever we are in a room together, I am in awe of how he phrases his statements to maximize clarity, impact, and forward movement. He can center everyone even when things get erratic. I want to develop those skills, so I want to be around him to learn as much as I can. What do you want to develop and who have you identified that models this behavior?

Availability and Dedication: Once, I started building a mentoring relationship with a senior banker. Each time I scheduled a meeting, her assistant rescheduled at least three times before we met, and when I was finally in her office, she was distracted by phone calls and emails. After three sessions, I knew she was unavailable to me, even with the best intentions. We are still very close today and she advises me on the fringes, but we don't have a formal mentoring relationship. Many people want to be helpful but have limited availability. Your inner circle will be available to you and dedicated to supporting you.

Quality of Advice: Your inner circle must provide high-quality advice that is honest, authentic, and given with empathy. Regardless of how much research you do beforehand, you will understand a mentor more when you start interacting with them. After each meeting, reflect on how that advice made you feel. Mentorship should be supportive, encouraging, and empowering. Consequently, ensure your mentor listens to your concerns and responds by sharing authentic stories and actionable strategies to help you grow.

We have discussed the importance of networks, the types of networks you should have, the qualities your networks must embody, some strategies for making connections, and what you need to do to deepen those connections into relationships as you and your career evolve.

Forming winning networks is not a talent reserved for those with an extroverted personality. Instead, this skill requires practice, and the earlier you begin your strategic and purposeful investment in your networks, the quicker they start generating results for you in your career and your life.

YOUR TURN!

1. List those in your core network and group your relationships into personal, operational, and strategic networks. Do your networks fit their purpose given the career aspirations you have?
2. Think about two or three abandoned relationships you want to revive. Using the SECURE framework, think about how you can reconnect and build again.

CHAPTER ELEVEN

Own Your Power

"Doubt kills more dreams than failure ever will."

—*Suzy Kassem*

****

Imagine going to the clinic with some mysterious pain you want diagnosed. The doctor completes their examination and says you may need an operation. However, at each step of the way, they second-guess themselves and question their decision. Would you feel safe in the care of a physician who doubts their judgment? Of course not!

Undoubtedly, trusting someone who doesn't trust themselves is hard. This also translates in the marketplace. The trust others have in what you can deliver is why they are willing to hire, pay, or promote you.

Another word for this trust is confidence. Confidence is the boldness and firm faith you have in your abilities. This refers to the sense that you can achieve what you have set out to do or the belief that you can create successful outcomes through your actions (Kay and Shipman, 2014).

In 2010, Cameron Anderson and Sebastien Brion, professors at the University of California, Berkeley, studied the relative value of confidence over competence. They concluded that individuals with overly positive self-perception of their abilities are more likely to attain higher status and influence in group environments. Using superficial cues like their nonverbal behavior, style of dressing, speaking, and physical characteristics, their peers also perceive their competence as superior.

You may have seen them: the people who lead discussions in meetings, give good presentations, and do not hesitate to share their views, whether popular or not. They are not necessarily the most competent in the room, but they are high on the confidence spectrum, which affords them more respect and influence.

Perception is king, and in the battle between competence and confidence, the latter wins nearly every time.

Unfortunately, despite 99 percent of the global workforce admitting that confidence is a critical skill, 79 percent of women and 62 percent of men admit to experiencing a lack of confidence in the workplace, which is holding them back from progressing in their careers (My Confidence Matters, 2019). For this reason, we cannot talk about contributing value without addressing this topic.

SOURCES OF CONFIDENCE

Where does confidence come from?

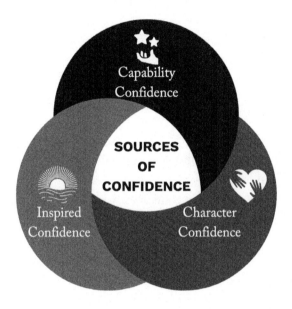

In episode 386 of *The Confidence Podcast*, titled, "How to Exude Confidence," host Trish Blackwell—athlete and internationally recognized confidence coach as well as founder of the College of Confidence—discusses two sources of confidence: capability confidence and character confidence.

CAPABILITY CONFIDENCE

This confidence stems from what you can do. You believe that you can create a successful outcome through your actions because you have done it before, giving you evidence to support your confidence.

- Do you have the knowledge, skills, and experience required to be successful where you are?
- Are you willing to try new things to build your experience?
- When confronted with a problem, can you think of a possible solution?
- Are you resourceful enough to handle unforeseen situations?

In my fifteen-year career, I have grown in confidence as a finance professional through my experience. When I get a phone call from my deal origination teams on a new investment opportunity, I am confident that I can understand the transaction risks and advise on how we could restructure the transaction to increase the chance of approval. If they approach me with a deal with unique characteristics that I have not seen before, I am confident that I can think critically, ask questions, learn what I don't know, and connect the dots.

You may be able to recall situations in which you did not feel confident in the face of a challenging task. Maybe it was driving, cooking a meal, leading a project, or starting a business. You may have hesitated, asked many questions, or experienced difficulty making decisions. But as you began taking action you felt your capability grow, and consequently, your confidence as well. When you produce good results, you feel more confident that you can repeat the outcomes if faced with the same situation. Even when things don't work out as planned, you will leave those experiences with lessons you can apply in future.

You can cultivate and enhance your capability confidence by repetition, skill expansion, keeping records of past successes, and receiving positive feedback. The more experience you gain, the more confident you feel.

This type of confidence is valuable but not sufficient by itself. As successful outcomes and positive feedback reinforce capability confidence, one bad experience or negative feedback can lower it. Character confidence can fill in the gaps when this happens.

CHARACTER CONFIDENCE

This confidence stems from who you are rather than what you do. This confidence is cultivated and enhanced by your upbringing, exposure, self-talk, and spiritual beliefs, and it is reflected in how you feel about yourself and understand your positioning in the world.

- How do you rate your chances of success?
- Are you optimistic or pessimistic about the future?
- Are you kind to yourself, or do you constantly criticize yourself?
- Do you internalize failure and condemn yourself at every step of the way?

Bozoma (Boz) Saint John is a marketing and branding powerhouse. She is a Ghanaian American woman who has held senior roles at Netflix, Pepsi, Apple, Uber, and Endeavour. In 2016, Boz walked into an Apple Worldwide Developers Conference (WWDC) standing six feet tall in a pink dress with a full afro to deliver her keynote speech on a newly launched Apple Music product.

As she demonstrated the product, she "got the party started" by playing The Sugarhill Gang's "Rapper's Delight." She shared the music and radio shows she loved, made her audience laugh, and even danced off the stage to Ghanaian Afrobeats. In five minutes and fifty seconds, she delivered a clear technical presentation with powerful presence. Her presentation was confidence personified. BuzzFeed even dubbed her "the coolest person to ever go on stage at an Apple event."

During an interview with *Fortune* magazine, Boz credited her confidence to her upbringing. Just before she turned thirteen, she moved to Colorado Springs with her family. She was six feet tall and weighed about one hundred pounds. "There was no choice. I couldn't hide. It was impossible anyway. I just couldn't be anything else, and so it meant that I had to become everything that I am," she said. "At thirteen, I learned what it meant to walk into a room and not care when everybody else turned around and looked at you."

Reflecting on that infamous Apple Music presentation, Boz shared that even though others with more experience advised her on the "acceptable" way of doing technical presentations, she decided to do it her way. "The only way to succeed is to do it your way. No one wants you to fail. However, they don't know the way that you should do it. I felt it necessary only to do it my way because I knew that was the way I would win, and I did win. I was the coolest person who ever walked on the Apple stage." Like Boz, your ability to show up authentically is one of the most tangible signs of character confidence.

As far as analogies go, it's a mystery which of these two forms of confidence is the chicken or the egg. Which one comes first? Either way, character confidence and capability confidence are equally important and should be cultivated. Different situations will require one or both to be present.

At a conference for women in leadership hosted by Girlboss, Boz boasted, "I am the best, and I challenge you to find a better marketer than me!" This statement bears such boldness, power, and exactness. And why not? Boz has a track record of projects that shows off her ability to execute and achieve relevant results. Even with her style, she is unapologetic about her clothes, long colorful nails, and "big" hair. In a world where Black women are often censored and told to conform to a standard of professionalism, Boz shows up like a ball of fire and captivates everyone in her presence.

That is not to say confidence must be gregarious and larger than life. It can also be quiet and assertive. For example, Indra Nooyi—the ex-chairperson and CEO of PepsiCo— always has a calm disposition when speaking and demonstrating extensive knowledge about her business at PepsiCo. She is an innovative risk-taker willing to share her opinion even when it's unpopular. She knows and understands her communication superpower and skillfully wields it in every conversation with admirable humor and wit. Hers is just as palpable as Boz's expression of her confidence, but it looks different.

Confidence is less about expression and more about what you believe or trust in yourself.

I recall when I had to lead my first client review meeting. I was six years into my role, and I had recently achieved promotion to vice president. Until then, I was only a secondary portfolio manager (PM). Even when I did most of the work on an account, senior staff always led the coverage. However, I no longer had that air cover in my elevated role, and I was now the primary or lead PM.

Of course, I panicked. But knowing there was no way out, I had to rely on what I knew to be true about myself.

- **My capabilities**: I had not led a diligence session before, but I had attended a few and understood the protocols. I knew the client well, given that I was the one who had written a few investment memos for them in the past. I knew that I possessed solid financial literacy, commercial awareness, and critical thinking skills that would help me understand the discussion on financial performance and key risks. I knew I had strong verbal communication skills and the gift of the gab to help me break the ice and have an engaging conversation with the client.
- **My character**: You may have observed that I am very self-assured and grounded in my belief that I can learn and do anything I put my mind to. I developed this belief through my upbringing as well as my Christian faith. I believe that I can do everything through Christ, who gives me strength (Holy Bible, Philippians 4:13 NLT). This belief is an anchor for me and helps me challenge myself daily.

In the end, my awareness of my character and related capabilities gave me the confidence to face the meeting, which went very well.

INSPIRED CONFIDENCE

Throughout my career, I have observed another source of confidence that is typically underestimated.

Sometimes, you may not have evidence of a successful outcome to rely on or even believe that you can achieve a goal you have set for yourself, but you can borrow confidence from those who believe in you or have done it before. I call this **inspired confidence**.

Motivators and role models are pivotal at various stages of your life. These people inspire action in you or role model the success that you want to achieve. They show you what is possible and provide a blueprint of how you can reach the same success.

When I wanted to start my company viSHEbility, I was skeptical about whether it would work. *Will people book my services? Will those I serve find it transformational? How will I manage my time?* I repeatedly asked myself these questions.

I shared my idea with a trusted friend, Jessica Ali. She encouraged me, telling me about how our informal pep talks had helped her in her career. She reminded me of how much I was already doing in the training and development space and how I was a natural speaker and teacher.

She also sent me a link to May Busch, a banker turned executive leadership coach. As I researched Busch, I found that she was a corporate leader who leveraged her expertise to build a coaching practice. I was inspired, and I knew I had to meet her. I emailed her and asked for a call. She agreed.

During this meeting, she said one thing to me that I will never forget. She said, "Do not despise what you know. Even your lowest level of insight is a bright light in the tunnel of someone else's confusion. You only need to coach to your level of competence. Those you serve will thank you for it." Wow, what a refreshing perspective.

I left that meeting feeling less anxious and more optimistic that there was a way forward. I borrowed confidence from Jessica's belief in me and May's evidence of success and inspiring words.

Who inspires you? Who believes in you? Let them speak life into you and fill your mind with possibilities.

CULTIVATE CONFIDENCE

If confidence is the belief that you can create successful outcomes through your actions, then a lack of confidence manifests when you doubt that you can. If confidence is self-assurance, then lack of confidence is self-doubt.

About ten years ago, I was petrified about presenting to an audience of more than one person. However, by intentionally cultivating confidence, I now speak to groups of all sizes at work and in my business. I went from not being able to talk to speaking for a living.

I also recall that when I was in university, I believed I could not write long pieces of work. At school, I shied away from courses that required long essays or dissertations. Thankfully, my degrees were more statistical than literary, and the lengthiest piece of work I wrote was five thousand words. Only my limiting belief held me back. However, by intentionally cultivating confidence, I have written lengthy financing proposals, training materials, and every single one of the sixty-seven thousand words that make up this book.

Although you may think that confidence is an attribute you either have or don't, "a substantial part of the confidence code is what psychologists call *volitional*: our choice. With diligent effort, we can all choose to expand our confidence." (Kay and Shipman, 2014)

Through my own experience, I have seen that no matter how low you are on the confidence scale, you can take deliberate actions to cultivate confidence by dealing with self-doubt that often comes from your fears and your limiting beliefs.

To begin dealing with your self-doubt, I have found this four-step **USER framework** beneficial to apply. For the rest of this chapter, we will look at the first half of the framework and complete the rest in the next chapter.

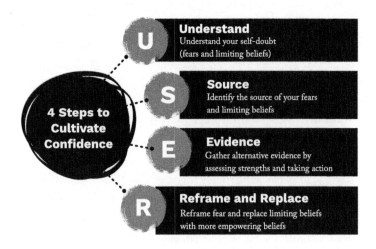

4 Steps to Cultivate Confidence

U — Understand
Understand your self-doubt
(fears and limiting beliefs)

S — Source
Identify the source of your fears
and limiting beliefs

E — Evidence
Gather alternative evidence by
assessing strengths and taking action

R — Reframe and Replace
Reframe fear and replace limiting beliefs
with more empowering beliefs

STEP ONE: UNDERSTAND YOUR FEARS AND LIMITING BELIEFS

The mind is the epicenter of decision-making and action-taking. Thoughts come first, followed by our words, which eventually determine our actions. To acknowledge your strengths, manifest big dreams, set goals, and contribute value, you need effective tactics for winning in the battlefield of your mind.

Our fears and limiting beliefs determine how we set goals for ourselves, make decisions, and approach learning new skills and exploring interests. They drive your actions, and actions drive your outcomes.

Fear comes from various sources and manifests itself in our behavior. In my experience, these behaviors come from three different fear sources.

1. **The fear of not knowing enough.** When you feel that your knowledge or skills are insufficient to lead you to

success, you overthink, prepare more than necessary due to anxiety, censor yourself and your contributions, and shy away from opportunities.

2. **The fear of not having enough.** When you fear losing what you have to other people, you might resort to clinging to your comfort zone, hesitating to make decisions, and being overly competitive.

3. **The fear of not being enough.** When you don't want to own your contributions because you don't think you deserve to, you might resort to internalizing setbacks, underselling your skills, apologizing too much, paranoia about people's perception of you, and overcompensating.

We all have triggers and patterns of behavior related to fear. I exhibit many of these behaviors at work.

A habit I just can't get rid of is overthinking and preparing more than necessary. I always want to know every detail because I never want to be in a position where I can't answer a question. I also cling to my comfort zone when I have the choice, and I undersell my skills occasionally. The key is to be aware of your triggers so you can identify them when they rear their ugly heads.

Limiting beliefs go hand in hand with fear. These are the negative thoughts or stories we consciously or unconsciously tell ourselves. They influence our view of our ability and right to achieve a particular goal, restricting us from doing the things we want or telling us that we don't deserve a certain level of success.

Do any of these limiting beliefs sound familiar?

- I don't have the right qualifications.
- I don't have enough experience.
- They would never promote someone like me.
- They can never pay me that much money.
- My boss doesn't like me.
- It's unlikely that I would be as successful as they are.

I remember my second day back on the Lancaster University campus for the start of the second year of my undergraduate degree. As customary at the beginning of the new year, I went to my faculty office to select my units for the year. My strategy was to choose the accounting courses that would get me the most exemptions from the post-graduation professional certification exams.

While in the queue, I started exchanging notes with my colleagues who were there for the same exercise. I showed them my selections, and one of them quickly said, "Don't select ACF212. I hear only 20 percent of the class pass that unit."

Momentary concern flashed in my mind. *I don't want to fail a unit. Let me look for an easier course*, I thought. My plan had met its first layer of resistance: my mindset.

When I couldn't take the confusion anymore, I called my dad and explained my dilemma. After listening to me think aloud for about ten minutes, he responded.

"Why are you not part of the 20 percent? Young lady, think yourself higher."

I was silent. This thought had not crossed my mind.

Why was I not confident in my ability to achieve what only a minority of students apparently could? Why did I not consider myself part of that minority? Why had I started panicking without considering how combining my knowledge, skills, attributes, history, and interests could improve the probability of passing that course?

My father encouraged me not to count myself out before even trying.

Without consulting anyone else, I submitted my course selections without any changes and left.

Not only did I pass that course, but I scored an A. My father's advice was what I needed to hear at that moment and, in fact, became my North Star through that course, the rest of my university experience, and my career.

Whenever you face a new challenge—a new client, a new project, or a new job—and you feel self-doubt creeping up, take the time to pay attention to your thoughts and ask clarifying questions to confirm your assumptions.

Say, for example, that you read a job description and immediately think you will not get the job, or you meet someone for the first time and assume they don't like you. Rather than ignoring your thoughts, you need to address them head-on. Ask yourself the following questions:

- Is there evidence that supports or negates this fear or belief?
- Why am I thinking the way I am right now?

- What am I afraid of?
- Why do I think I will not produce a successful outcome through my actions?

Of course, there could be times when you may not find evidence to invalidate the existence of your self-doubt. For example, if you accept a project manager job but don't have the necessary skills, experience, or qualifications, your fear and limiting beliefs about your ability to succeed are valid until you do what is needed to equip yourself for that job. In any case, asking these questions will ensure that your assumptions are grounded in fact, not fiction.

You must also acknowledge the opportunity cost of holding to your fears and limiting beliefs by asking:

- What do I have to gain?
- Am I willing to miss out on this opportunity?
- What will I leave on the table? Will it be recognition, more money, increased visibility, influence, or something else?

The truth is that self-doubt always costs us something. When you can assess that, you give yourself the push you need to overcome your fears and press forward.

STEP TWO: IDENTIFY THE SOURCE OF THE FEARS AND LIMITING BELIEFS

Fears and limiting beliefs come from external messages we hear in the world, whether from childhood, school, work, media, observing other people, or our personal experiences.

Especially when we experience adverse outcomes, we begin to internalize those outcomes as rules which form our worldview.

I have experienced this as well. When I started work, I observed a pattern of behavior in myself that I did not like. I was generally comfortable sharing my opinions with my peer and junior teammates, but once a senior-level staff member walked into the room, I clammed up. I was shy to ask questions or offer a dissenting opinion. My inability to challenge meant failing at a core function of my job as a risk manager.

I later did a brainstorming exercise with the help of a coach, which helped me identify a limiting belief behind this behavior and where that belief came from.

"Why do you clam up?" she asked.

"I'm shy, and I don't want to say the wrong thing," I replied.

"I don't think you are shy. So, let's try that again. Why?"

"I think it is disrespectful."

"Why?"

"Because they are older and more experienced."

"So what?"

"They must know more than I do and be correct. Why would I want to argue?"

"Why do you think they know more?"

"Isn't this always the case? Elders know more."

"Where did you hear that?"

"That's how it is in my culture. Older people call the shots, and you must not challenge them."

Bingo! I had identified the belief and its source.

I realized that my culture and upbringing had not done me any favors in this regard. In the Nigerian school system, teachers were like demigods. They taught us what we needed to know and were not open to being challenged. This behavior followed the societal norm. Elders were supposed to be the wisdom whisperers and fountains of all knowledge. I even know an adage that supports this: "An adult can see from the ground what a child cannot see even when standing on a tree." At home, the expectation was no different. When my parents' friends visited, I left the room because children were not present when adults conversed. Even if I stayed, I was not to contribute to the discussion.

All this seemed harmless till I got to the workplace and started having the problems I've described. As you think about your fears and limiting beliefs, do not ignore how your familial and environmental factors can impact your professional life, both positively and negatively. You must dig deep into some areas that may seem normal to you. If you need to, engage a trained therapist or a life coach.

Once you identify your fears and limiting beliefs in step one, you must also identify their source by asking where and who they came from. Where did I hear that? Who told me that?

Once I understood my limiting belief and identified its source, I had to do the work to replace that belief. Over the years, I have learned that elders are not always right and that age doesn't equal wisdom. I had to enforce that reality in my mind consciously. I also reinforced the importance of using my voice and the personal and professional implications of not speaking up.

It takes a continuous effort to rewire my brain to hold more empowering beliefs in this regard, but I recognize the progress I have made. I am constantly challenging the status quo now, proving that you, too, can replace thoughts and patterns of behavior.

YOUR TURN!

1. Pick a goal or challenge for your future progression. For example, you could choose a career goal you have set for yourself, a barrier holding you back from progressing, or a skill you want to master.
2. Reflect on these questions:
   - What fears are holding you back from pursuing this goal?
   - What are your limiting beliefs about your ability or right to achieve this goal?
   - What are your helpful beliefs about your ability or right to achieve this goal?

- Where has that fear or limiting belief come from? Can you pinpoint the experience(s) which led to it?
- What is a fact? What is interpretation? How do you know something is true?

CHAPTER TWELVE

Respond to Self-Doubt

"Good Thinking = Good Choices = Healthy Thoughts;
Toxic Thinking = Toxic Choices = Toxic Thoughts"
—Dr. Caroline Leaf

****

We all have voices in our heads. For some, the voices are comforting and provide guidance. For others, the voices are scary and overwhelming. Regardless of what they say, they are just thoughts. How you respond either strengthens or weakens their power over you.

If you allow yourself to continue thinking negative or unproductive thoughts, they will consume your day and take you down the wrong path. But if you allow yourself to think happy and hopeful thoughts, they will empower you and take you where you want to go.

Unfortunately, like many people, you may not know how to take control of your negative thoughts. Do you try to ignore or block them out? Do you do what they tell you to do?

CULTIVATE CONFIDENCE (PART TWO)

After you have understood your fears and limiting beliefs and identified their source (see Chapter Eleven), your next steps are to gather alternative evidence, reframe your fears, and replace your limiting beliefs.

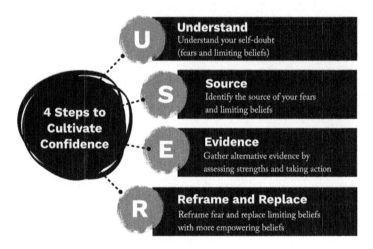

4 Steps to Cultivate Confidence

U — Understand
Understand your self-doubt
(fears and limiting beliefs)

S — Source
Identify the source of your fears
and limiting beliefs

E — Evidence
Gather alternative evidence by
assessing strengths and taking action

R — Reframe and Replace
Reframe fear and replace limiting beliefs
with more empowering beliefs

STEP THREE: GATHER ALTERNATIVE EVIDENCE

If you read or listen to the stories of some of the most visibly successful people, you will observe that they all feel fear and self-doubt. What sets them apart is what they do with that.

Michelle Obama is a great example. As an attorney with degrees from Princeton University and Harvard Law School and as the former First Lady of the United States (FLOTUS), one would assume that someone like her doesn't struggle with self-doubt. However, she revealed the opposite to be true in an interview with British newspaper *The Sunday Times*.

Michelle was nervous the night before her book *Becoming* was released. To kick off her global book tour, she was scheduled for a live interview with Oprah Winfrey, which would be held in front of fourteen thousand people. "I lay awake anxious in my bed, worried that these little stories couldn't bear the enormous load," she confessed. "What if the book just isn't any good? What if people hate it? Or what if they just don't care?" You may have been there; I certainly have.

Thankfully, her husband, Barack, was on hand to give her a boost of confidence. "Barack put his arms around me and placed his forehead on mine. 'It's good, Miche,' he told me. 'It really is,'" she said. He reminded her of all the work she had done in her career before, during, and after becoming FLOTUS. He helped her reconnect with her strengths and the value she has delivered in the past.

With these words in mind, Michelle stepped on stage the next day and in the days that followed. According to *Forbes*, Michelle Obama's book sold more copies than any other book in the United States in 2018. By March 2019, the book sold fourteen million copies worldwide (New York Times, 2019). As she reflected on her experience, she said, "We all have our tender spots, and our instinct is to keep them protected.

This book affirmed within me the value in bucking against that instinct and stepping into our fears" (Obama, 2021).

Michelle's story highlights the two effective ways of responding to your fears and limiting beliefs. You need to reconnect with your strengths, and you need to take action.

RECONNECT WITH YOUR STRENGTHS

Reconnecting with your strengths is about reminding yourself that you are capable and of what you have in your arsenal to succeed in your current situation. Do the following in order to reconnect with your strengths:

1. **Capitalize on your strengths.** Revisit Part One of this book. Review your list of strengths and which ones will be the most helpful for what you are working to achieve.

2. **Reflect on your past achievements.** Let them serve as a reminder of the value you have contributed. "*Confidence* occurs when the *insidious* self-perception that you aren't able is trumped by the stark reality of your achievements." (Kay and Shipman, 2014) Cultivate the habit of keeping records of your past successes. When you get a thank-you email, a testimonial, or a great performance review, keep it. These serve as evidence of your capabilities, which you should refer to in moments of self-doubt.

3. **Surround yourself with people who actually boost your confidence, and eliminate those who do not.** In Chapter Eleven, we looked at the importance of motivators and role models to inspire action in you.

TAKING ACTION

After doing this internal work, feed bravery by taking action toward what you haven't done before. You need to feel the fear and do it anyway.

Confidence is a muscle that gets stronger as you take action. Taking action means applying for that job, sending the proposal, speaking up in that meeting, saying yes to the project or opportunity to present, joining that new team, and so on. It also means practicing, preparing, and closing your skills gaps. Doing what you haven't done before is the only way to make it something you have done. This is the only way to prove to yourself that you can learn new things and you can execute.

Oluchi Ikechi-D'Amico (Oli for short) has had an extensive and successful career in consulting and professional services. She achieved partner status within ten years of entering the workplace and was one of the youngest partners at Accenture. Among the many things she credits for her rapid ascent in her career, she places her ability to take action even when she didn't feel fully equipped at the top of the list.

Oli shared a story about when her manager took a leave of absence, which left her inheriting his client portfolio and the team. "I found myself in a position where I could make my own decisions," she reflects. "Yes, I could ask for help when I needed to, but the power to decide what makes good, practical, and logical sense laid with me."

She was doing everything from pricing deals to reviewing contracts. She was also learning how to communicate better and more effectively, and the difference between managing and leading a team. "It was all a learning experience," she says. "This was when I realized that the managers I looked up to are not perfect; they just have more experience through which they developed skills, capabilities, and intuition." Her expanded new role afforded her the same potential to gain experience, as she often found herself outside her comfort zone.

"Being on my own was great. It gave me the springboard that I needed," Oli says. "The more I did something unfamiliar, the more I became familiar with it." This motivated Oli to think up new business ideas, and she began expanding the remit of her responsibilities from one project to another. She focused on developing her thought leadership and building internal capabilities to store knowledge so she could better advise her clients. "I was moving away from being just a consultant to being a consultant with a point of view. I realized that the more I developed my point of view and shared it, even if it was wrong or right, the more I felt people were listening. The more I entertained dialogue and discussion, my point of view became richer. So, I kept going and gained more confidence."

Today, Oli continues to thrive in her career and is currently a partner at Ernst & Young, where she heads strategy and transaction capital markets in the Asia-Pacific region.

When you take action, you create more results and learn more. This grows your capability, which builds your confidence and perpetuates a new cycle of more action, more confidence, and more results.

In the words of the world-famous painter Vincent van Gogh, "If you hear a voice within you say, 'You cannot paint,' then by all means paint, and that voice will be silenced."

STEP FOUR: REFRAME FEAR AND REPLACE LIMITING BELIEFS

Reconnecting with your strengths and taking action does not mean that you will not feel doubt anymore. It just means you will no longer let that feeling hold you back.

Caring about what other people think is normal. Fearing what could go wrong over what could go right is normal (remember the human negativity bias discussed in Chapter Two?). Trying to keep a past adverse scenario recurring in your future is normal. But the fear behind all of this must be reframed in order to be stripped of its power.

REFRAME FEAR

When it comes to fear, I have come to appreciate it. Here's why:

- Fear is a survival instinct that stops you from entering dangerous territory. Imagine going about your life without awareness of what could harm you? Fear will cause you to pause, think, and strategize, which can only be helpful.
- Fear shows that you care about the outcome and is an excellent motivator to do the work necessary to avoid failure. It forces you to prepare. When doctors are about to operate, they go over the procedure repeatedly as preparation. When you are about to take a test, you

(hopefully!) study. Bozoma Saint John said it best: "If you want to achieve something, preparing for that eventual happening is what's going to make sure you succeed. It's not about spontaneity and just getting up and going, because you need to understand what it will take, the risks, and how you overcome those things."

- Fear opens you up to external advice. When working on a big project, I call my mentors and advisers to seek guidance. I know that "without wise leadership, a nation falls; there is safety in having many advisers" (Holy Bible; Proverbs 11:14 NLT).

- Fear is a sign that you are growing intentionally. The feeling of fear is a stretching feeling, which means that you are taking risks, growing, challenging yourself, and building your capacity. You must be stretched if you want to develop professionally.

These reframed ways of thinking about fear will help you consider it a faithful friend that shows up at the most critical times of your career and life. Listen to what the fear might be able to teach you, but don't let it get in your way.

REPLACING LIMITING BELIEFS

Limiting beliefs, on the other hand, require a different approach. When a belief limits success, you must replace it with more empowering and productive beliefs. Beliefs are just stories we tell ourselves, not facts, and if a story is no longer serving you, you can always change that story. In other words, if a thought enters your head that says, "I am not smart enough," you can respond by saying, "Oh yes, I am." This will induce you to think differently about yourself.

This method of rewriting is also known as neuroplasticity, which refers to "the brain's ability to modify, change, and adapt both structure and function throughout life and in response to experience." (Voss, Thomas et al., 2017)

In her book *Switch on Your Brain*, Dr. Caroline Leaf says that "you can, through conscious effort, gain control of your thoughts and feelings, and in doing so, you can change the programming and chemistry of your brain." She went further to say that "as we think, we change the physical nature of our brain. As we consciously direct our thinking, we can wire out toxic patterns of thinking and replace them with healthy thoughts."

Positive daily affirmations are a widely accepted method of brain rewiring. When you dwell on good thoughts and repeat them, they will combat subconscious patterns and replace them with more adaptive narratives.

In their book *Will It Make The Boat Go Faster?*, Ben Hunt-Davis and Harriet Beveridge share four helpful beliefs to cultivate if we want to activate our self-belief toward achieving our goals. An easy way to remember this framework is **DICE**: I deserve this, it's important, I can, and it's exciting.

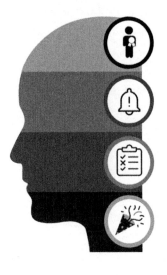

I DESERVE this
- I am good enough
- I am worthy (of love/respect/success...)

It's IMPORTANT
- The benefits are...
- This will give me...
- This will help me to...

I CAN do it
- I can figure it out
- I can get help where needed
- I can build it, sell it, write it, do it

It's EXCITING
- What's good about this is...
- I will be so proud when I have achieved this...
- I will enjoy learning to...
- This could also lead to...

I Deserve This

I remember a student I mentored in 2017. During one of our sessions, I asked questions about her academic journey. She told me that she had decided to attend a C-level university in London instead of a Russell Group university in the Midlands because her mum wanted her to stay closer to home. I was surprised by the advice and by her decision.

She had the qualifying grades needed to attend a prestigious university, and she had no reason to be close to home except her mum's wish. Did she not know the brand equity of attending a Russell Group university? Did she not do her research or speak to informed people before making her decision?

As we dug deeper into her past, we uncovered a string of instances when she could have pursued more for herself in life but chose not to. In a flood of tears, she recounted how her student counselor told her, "People like you don't go to places like that," and then suggested that she try local universities instead of league schools.

Being a Black woman myself, the meaning of that statement was apparent to me, as was the impact it could have on a young person's formative mindset and confidence. That singular decision not to pursue attendance at a more prestigious university had a negative effect on this student's ability to access jobs early on in her career because, sadly, we still live in an age where your alma mater has the potential to advance or slow down your career prospects.

Unfortunately, this young lady is one of many people who have bought the lie that they did not deserve what was within reach at different points in their education and career. I see young professionals who shy away from doing hard things because of certain beliefs they have harbored and held to be true about the likely outcome of a particular choice. Every year, many students, especially those from ethnic minority backgrounds, choose not to apply to top-ranking universities because they don't see themselves in those spaces. The problem is not that they didn't get in but that they didn't even try.

The solution for this particular student was to expose herself to the positive influence of industry mentors. We collectively started challenging these limiting beliefs and telling her that she deserved a vision of the future she wanted for herself.

By sharing our own authentic stories, she started to form a picture of what could be possible. She now saw that people like her could and do exist in the spaces she wanted to be in.

Today, she has a thriving career in financial services and works for a tier-one investment bank that would typically not recruit from a non-Russell Group university. She finally believed that she could, and so she did.

A voice will always challenge whether you are worthy to even aim for what you want—*How dare you! Who do you think you are?*—but you have to believe that you are worthy and deserving of success. You deserve to attend a top school. You deserve to get that job. You deserve to earn more. You deserve that promotion. You deserve the vision of the future that you want for yourself.

It's Important

Councilor Sabrina Francis was appointed the mayor of Camden, London, United Kingdom in May 2021. She is the first Black woman to serve as a labor councilor and be appointed mayor in the council's history. Alongside for- ty-two other councilors, her role is to represent her ward and the people who live in it. Councilors develop council policy, get involved in planning and regulation, serve as community leaders, and provide a bridge between the diverse community and the council.

Speaking about why she decided to run for council, Sabrina said, "I think it important to have a variety of people on council because we have different experiences, knowledge, and interests. Our decision-making could be different but is strengthened when we come together."

Sabrina recalled an incident when she sat on a committee that gives out licenses to bars, clubs, and restaurants to enable them to sell alcohol. Typically, a review process unfolds if an establishment has done something wrong. Through researching the history of over-policing events at the expense of "urban" communities (meaning Black communities), in which the police used obscure parts of the licensing rules to unjustly penalize people of color, Sabrina realized she was in the prime position to speak up against discriminatory behavior. She said, "During the review, the police were in attendance to share their experience with the venue and provide an objective view, but I could see how they were talking about it, and I knew that their narrative was laced with racial prejudice. I knew that I had to speak up. It was important."

She challenged the use of loopholes in the licensing rules. "I don't think the other people on the committee would have known the history of the over-policing of urban events, but I knew that because I am Black and I actively read news stories about issues affecting the Black community. Being in that room was important to ensure that the council made the decision fairly."

If you don't think achieving your goal is important, if you don't think your presence or voice is meaningful, or if you don't believe that you can have significant impact, then no one else will. As you think about your career—whether that means taking up a new job, speaking up in a meeting, asking

for a pay raise, or asking for a new project or more resources—
ask yourself:

- What are the benefits? What positive change can I
  create if I achieve this?
- What is the opportunity cost? What are the consequences and repercussions if I don't take this action?
- Who would be positively impacted by my decision to
  just go for it?

The answers to these questions will show just how important
your pursuit is. They will help you craft the story in your mind
that your voice, presence, and actions can make a difference.
Focusing on this new story will energize you when times get
tough and you want to give up or stay quiet. You will know
that what you are doing or about to embark on is important.

I Can Do This

"I am a salesperson. I cannot do strategy," said Tina, a business development manager at one of the leading technology
firms in the world. For the first eleven years of her career, she
worked within the client sales function, closing software and
hardware deals with some of the largest companies in Africa.
She eventually decided to take on a new career challenge by
pivoting into business development, which involves more
strategic thinking than sales execution work.

At first, she was excited about the opportunity, and then
she got in her head about it. Despite evidence of her ability
to succeed, Tina panicked every time she had a strategy
meeting. Tongue-tied, she sat in the room and left without

any valuable contribution. Of course, it began to impact her team's perception of her contribution.

Eventually, her manager recognized the issue and sent her for some leadership coaching. She explained to her coach that she had always been in sales and didn't feel she had what it took to create a business strategy for a client. Acknowledging this limiting belief, her coach probed further. "What is strategy?"

"It is how we will solve the client's problem by using the firm's products or services," Tina replied.

"Pick a client and tell me what their problem is."

"It is a South African company that wants to increase its brand awareness and name recognition with their start-up customers in Nigeria."

"So what solutions can your company provide to help them solve this problem?"

"We have search engine ads to improve online visibility in their target market. We also have connections with the start-up community in Nigeria, so we can help them host virtual events that would mutually benefit all parties involved. We also have a dedicated start-up manager who can connect them with those who will have other ideas."

"See, Tina, you can do strategy!"

By breaking down the issue for Tina and allowing her to speak freely in a safe environment, Tina was more relaxed and answered the question. She was no longer in her head and proved that she could think critically and generate ideas. She also figured out how to leverage her core relationship-building strength to engage other team members to support the work.

Tina learned this lesson with some challenges, but you don't have to. Sometimes the thought that you cannot do something exists because of complexity which needs to be untangled. You need to simplify and clarify. Just like Tina, get out of your head.

Take a pen and paper, write out the problem, start breaking it down into parts, and solve each piece. While doing this, believe that you can find a solution. As Henry Ford said, "Whether you believe you can or you can't, you are probably right." Change the question from "Can I do this?" to "How will I do this?"

The former raises a question about your ability and seeks permission to be allowed to do it. The latter is a more empowering question that starts from the point of possibility rather than permission. What I'm doing is possible. I can do this, but I need to figure out how. I need to have a plan. I need to find the right people. I need to connect the various dots, and I will hit the mark once I do.

You can do whatever you set your mind to.

It's Exciting

In 2018, I was approached by a global investment bank to join their credit risk team as an executive director. At this point, I had been at BoA for ten years and was a vice president six months away from being promoted to director. I enjoyed my role and the people I worked with. I had the support of senior people and endless opportunities in my functional role and across the firm.

That said, I had been at BoA all my career. I knew I had become too comfortable in my seat and started getting that unsettling feeling that comes with knowing you need to shake things up. When this great opportunity came, I decided to go through the interview process.

A few weeks later, I got the call. "We would like to offer you the role."

I was elated, but then panic ensued. *What if I hate it? What if I don't like the people? What would happen to the people I managed and mentored? How would I explain this to my parents, managers, and sponsors? How can I give up all the goodwill I have built up in my ten years at BoA?*

I had so many questions. This led me to seek advice from a few peers and senior mentors. One particular conversation stood out to me. After rattling off all my objections, my friend asked me a straightforward question.

"Try to visualize two years into the future. Would you be better off if you stayed or made the change?"

I had not considered my decision in that light.

In answering that question, I could magnify the benefits of taking the job. This would refresh my career. I would be exploring risk management in a different context, have access to a different caliber of professionals, learn through the experience of transitioning and integrating into a new organization, and embrace the opportunity to be a leader and culture carrier in a new sphere of influence.

The opportunity was more exciting than I thought. Of course, I would miss my colleagues and the firm I had grown up in, but I trusted the relationships that mattered to me would be maintained even if I left. As long as I handled my departure well, I could retain the goodwill and trust I had built over the years.

I took the job. Doing so was not easy. Some of my fears materialized, but so did the wins. I knew I would gain experience and learn more in my career because I made that move, and it proved to be the right decision. Knowing this helped me keep a positive attitude when inevitable challenges arose throughout the transition.

This experience taught me the power of making decisions based on what I could gain rather than what I might lose. Sometimes even if you stand to gain only one thing, it could outweigh all the things you think you are losing. You will lose things along the way as you transition through life, but you lose things to make room for something better.

As George Addair said, "Everything you've ever wanted is sitting on the other side of fear." Whenever you fear doing something you have never done before—such as meeting people who are different from you or going to new places— rather than shrinking your future in your mind, consider the adventure that could unfold on the other side of your fears. Think about how much you will grow, how much you will learn, and how much your network will expand. This should be exciting, not just scary. Focusing on the possibilities will help you get over your temporary discomfort.

Whenever a limiting belief comes in to challenge your right and ability to achieve a goal, roll the DICE: you deserve this, it's important, you can do it, and it's exciting.

YOUR TURN!

1. Using the DICE framework, craft new, empowering beliefs to replace the limiting beliefs you have identified.

CHAPTER THIRTEEN

Prioritize Your Health

*"He who has health, has hope; and he
who has hope, has everything."*

—*Arabian Proverb*

****

Did you know that the average person will spend at least
90,000–115,000 hours at work over a lifetime? This excludes
the time taken to get ready and commute to and from your
place of work, and implies a significant amount of time spent
planning, executing tasks, maintaining your performance,
managing people, and delivering value for your stakeholders.

In their 1948 constitution, the World Health Organization
defined health as "a state of complete physical, mental and
social well-being and not merely the absence of disease or
infirmity." In other words, you do not have to be sick to be
in a poor state of health.

Health, or a lack thereof, can have a significant impact on
your productivity at work in a variety of ways.

1. **Health can affect your energy levels.** Your overall health directly impacts your energy levels. If you're feeling run-down and tired, it will be harder to focus and be productive. On the other hand, if you're feeling healthy and energized, you'll find it much easier to power through your work.

2. **Health can affect your mood.** If you're feeling down or stressed, motivating yourself to get started on tasks can be challenging. However, if you're in a good mood, you'll likely approach your work more positively and be more productive.

3. **Health can affect your focus.** When you're not feeling well, it can be hard to concentrate on your work. Headaches, nausea, and other physical symptoms can make it difficult to focus on anything else. Conversely, if you're feeling good, you'll be able to direct your attention to a task and be more productive.

I have experienced firsthand the effects of nonoptimal levels of health. On two occasions, I took relatively long absences (between two to four months) from work when my health needed to be prioritized. These incidents were in addition to the odd days off to recharge or recover from minor illnesses. Whenever my physical or mental health was not at its best, delivering optimal performance and contributing value was more challenging.

PHYSICAL HEALTH

Of the many things I have learned in my fifteen years in the workplace, one is that you have to be intentional about prioritizing your physical health.

Hustle culture, prevalent in this generation, might encourage you to work fourteen hours a day. In the bid to respond urgently to clients, do more with less, and balance side hustles, it often seems very little time is left to do anything else. Still, this culture doesn't tell you how to take care of yourself when that lifestyle lands you in a hospital bed ten years later.

I used to eat out constantly, usually grabbing the quickest high-fat or high-sugar meal within reach. I was eventually diagnosed with high cholesterol and prediabetes—news made worse by my familial history of diabetes. I had been eating the same way since I was young with no issues, but it seemed I had missed the memo that my metabolism would slow down as I got older.

Exercise also seemed inconvenient. I felt there was not enough time to get a good one-hour workout when I could spend that one hour doing more work. I was a member of many gyms but a visitor to none. Inevitably, I struggled to stay agile. Basic movements like running around or climbing stairs became a challenge. Again, this was worsened by my familial predisposition to arthritis.

And then there was sleep, or the lack thereof. Long stretches and late nights at work, aided by high caffeine and sugar consumption, made it difficult to get sufficient sleep. My workdays were mainly fueled by adrenaline. I was tired all the time, and I had headaches constantly. I started turning up to work late and could not focus throughout the day. My memory also became more porous. I was forgetful of things, quickly confused, and altogether not as productive as my stakeholders needed me to be.

My knees and back hurt from sitting for too long. My eyes were weakened by the glare from the screen and reading tiny print on due diligence materials. I eventually had to get reading glasses.

These are only a subset of the health issues I developed over my first eight years at work. The symptoms were initially unnoticeable, but eventually I started falling ill every other week. I knew that something had to give! I needed a better quality of life. I needed to show up to work actually feeling ready to work.

To do this, I had to stop leaving my health to chance. I set some SMARTER health goals and implemented an effective strategy. One of these was signing up for a health transformation program where I could leverage the accountability of a coach and personal trainer, as mentioned in Chapter Five.

We focused on nutrition, physical activity, hydration, and sleep. By the end of my program, I was sixteen kilograms lighter, free from joint pain, and sleeping like a baby. My posture got better as I improved my physique. My cholesterol and sugar levels normalized. My eyes and brain function improved. I observed an increase in my focus and productivity. I was less stressed and had more energy without reliance on caffeine and sugar. I got my groove back.

Aside from treating specific medical diagnoses, these physical health habits have significant benefits to productivity and your ability to contribute value.

1. **Good nutrition.** Eating nutrient-dense foods supported by vitamin supplements increases our ability to fight off and recover from illness or injury. Beyond that, good, nutritious food provides vitamins and nutrients the human brain needs in order to function correctly. When our brains are adequately fueled, this helps to increase cognitive function, concentration, energy, mood, and self-esteem (Hrechka and Woodley, 2021).
2. **Hydration.** According to Harvard Health (2017), drinking enough water helps to regulate body temperature, keep joints lubricated, prevent infections, deliver nutrients to cells, and keep organs functioning properly.
3. **Physical activity.** In 2010, Dr. Thomas Frieden, former director at the Centers for Disease Control and Prevention (CDC), dubbed physical activity 'the closest thing we have to a wonder drug' because of its numerous benefits. Regular physical activity has been proven to "reduce the risk of heart disease, diabetes, obesity, high blood pressure, stroke, depression, certain kinds of cancer, and premature death." (Warburton, Darren et al. 2006) CDC also said that physical activity has a tremendous effect on mental health. This is because of its impact on improved mood, sleep, thinking, learning, judgment, and reduced stress and anxiety.
4. **Sleep.** Often underestimated, this is one of the essential things we can do for our bodies and minds. Among its many benefits, quality sleep supports muscle growth and tissue repair, boosts our immune system, and improves heart health. According to Headspace, part

of Headspace Health, while asleep, our body gets the opportunity to repair and rejuvenate itself. I always find that when I have a good sleep, I generate new ideas and consolidate various thoughts I may have been struggling with during the day. Not getting enough sleep can also increase the risk of obesity and diabetes since we are more likely to make healthier food choices when well-rested.

Embarking on my physical health transformation taught me many lessons about health, and each one is also applicable to the rest of life.

- **Be intentional.** If I want to eat healthy and whole-some meals, I need to plan and prepare my meals over the weekend before the busy week starts. Similarly, if I want to make sure I exercise, I need to pay for the session ahead of time. Nothing encourages me to show up as much as the prospect of losing money.
- **Implement discipline over motivation.** Once I decide to work out four days a week, I have no excuses. I do not need to "feel" like it. I just need to show up and get the workout done.
- **Value progress over perfection.** I do not need to run a marathon or lift the heaviest barbell on the first day. However, if I start where I am, I can continue working toward getting faster and stronger every day.

I also saw how important it is to have regular checkups at least once a year. This way, you have a greater chance of uncovering hidden issues. One of those checkups revealed that my cholesterol levels were high, I was prediabetic, deficient in Vitamin D, and also anemic. I might not have known if I hadn't checked—perhaps until it was too late.

Setting SMARTER health goals around your number of weekly exercise sessions, the minimum hours of sleep you get per night, the quality of your food, and the frequency of medical checkups you get will support healthy living and optimal performance. Your goals should remain flexible enough to adapt to your age and other life demands.

MENTAL HEALTH

Between guarding your physical health and guarding your mental health, the greater challenge lies with mental health, which is the largest and fastest-growing category of the burden of disease worldwide, according to the World Health Organization (WHO). According to WHO, nearly one billion people are affected by mental health disorders ranging from anxiety and mood swings to diagnoses such as autism spectrum disorder, clinical depression, bipolar disorder, dementia, schizophrenia, and various psychoses.

We go through normal peaks and troughs with our mental health just as we do our physical health. But some peaks and troughs stand out more than the others. We usually label these "incidents."

While optimal mental health is often considered the absence of mental disorders or disabilities, WHO has broadened its scope to more than just their absence. "Mental health is a state of well-being in which an individual realizes his or her abilities, can cope with the normal stresses of life, can work productively, and can make a contribution to his or her community." (WHO, 2018)

In the workplace, burnout is one of the leading causes of mental illness. In 2019, burnout was formally included in the eleventh revision of the International Classification of Diseases as an occupational phenomenon (WHO, 2019). The handbook describes burnout as a syndrome that results from chronic workplace stress that has not been successfully managed.

Across the board, the statistics are frightening and worthy of attention. "1 in 6.8 people (14.7 percent) experience mental health problems in the workplace such as anxiety, panic attacks, depression, and post-traumatic stress disorder" (OECD, 2013). 76 percent of full-time employees report feeling burned out at work very often, always, or sometimes. Burned-out employees are 63 percent more likely to take a sick day and two-and-a-half times as likely to actively seek a different job. Even if they stay, they typically have 13 percent lower confidence in their performance (Gallup, 2019). Despite the dire statistics, as many as 80 percent of those with a common mental disorder do not seek or receive treatment (OECD, 2011).

Sadly, I have experienced the damaging effects of poor mental health on my life but was part of that 80 percent that didn't seek immediate help. In 2003, I moved to the UK from Nigeria at sixteen after my first breakup. In 2007, I graduated from university and entered the "real world" at age twenty. In 2014, I was stressed out from work and struggled to visualize my future at the age of twenty-seven. And in 2019 at the age of thirty-two, I suddenly lost my dad a few months after a significant transition in my career.

The first two seasons of difficulty came and went almost unnoticed, as most mental health issues do. Frankly, I was much younger and didn't have the language to define what I was going through. I just knew that I was sad and withdrawn all the time. I put it down to the experience of transitioning between countries initially, and later, I dismissed it as being due to transitioning into the workplace. Growing up in Nigeria had much to do with my ignorance on these matters. Mental illness was (and still is) a largely misunderstood, taboo subject. Even when spoken of, the discussion is full of cultural and religious rhetoric with no medical or scientific value, often stigmatizing the sufferer. With time, I just found a way to get out of my funk without seeking help. In hindsight, this is not the ideal approach. Ignoring your troughs can have damaging effects later on.

The third incident, however, was more severe. For a host of reasons, I had maintained a suboptimal pattern of working for most of my life, which eventually put me in a state of emotional, physical, and mental exhaustion. I had been in formal education since I was eight years old until I graduated from my master's program at twenty-one. I started my career in the global financial crisis, a traumatic five-year period of navigating change and loss. For the first four years of work, I studied part-time for the ACCA accountancy qualification without taking more than a ten-day break each year.

I was also managing the impact of my parents being diagnosed with chronic illness. My father was diagnosed with prostate cancer and had to undergo grueling radiotherapy. My mother was diagnosed with high blood pressure and hyperthyroidism, which required daily management. I was juggling my internal exhaustion and external triggers while also trying to cope with the pressures of a demanding job. In summary, I took on too much and was going through too much.

While I was a bit more informed about mental health living in a relatively open British society, I still chose to do nothing. Why? Well, for many reasons.

First, I was embarrassed. How could this be happening to me? I remember thinking, *I am strong! This doesn't and shouldn't happen to me.*

Second, I didn't feel I could speak out. My parents didn't understand or have language for it, so they couldn't help me navigate what I was experiencing, and they were already going through a lot. Both my parents were public sector veterans where the pace was much slower, and they didn't understand the pressures of UK private sector financial services.

Third, I suffered from the myth of gratitude. During the challenging economic period, I knew I was one of the lucky few who had a job straight out of school. With many of my friends still scouring the job market, I felt it would be ungrateful if I complained.

Fourth, I carried the burden of the minority. I felt I needed to be okay, otherwise "they" would say, "This is why we don't hire women or Black people." I felt that leaving would reinforce bias.

Fifth, I was on a sponsored working visa, so I couldn't risk losing my job. This is an additional burden that immigrants carry.

Six, that year was a pivotal promotion year for me. I worked hard to get to that point and didn't want to lose momentum.

Finally, I carried a reinforced sense of indispensability. Because I had been with the firm for a while, I had a false notion that everything would break if I was not here.

The straw finally broke the camel's back when I completed the ACCA and got my indefinite leave to remain in the UK in 2014. You might assume this would be a happy season for me, but it was quite the opposite. The adrenaline of seeing these two things to the finish line had been holding me up, and once they were gone, I came crashing down.

Eventually, I became physically ill and had to take medical leave for eight weeks. This confirms research by clinical psychologist Julie Fraga that "burnout can lower your immune system, making you more susceptible to colds, the flu, and insomnia."

Some of the symptoms I experienced included:

- Lack of motivation and difficulty concentrating
- Irritability or impatience with people
- Anxiety and inability to make decisions
- Hopelessness
- Overeating
- Insomnia (inability to sleep or sleep deeply)

- Physical illness symptoms like headaches, recurring infections, and low energy

With the help of a supportive manager and medical advice, I took the time I needed to rest. I lay in the sun, took my medication, slept for days, and took the time to clear my head. Slowly but surely, I started to feel rested, refreshed, and optimistic. I returned to work with renewed focus, improved decision-making capacity, and increased productivity. I understood what was important to me and what goals I wanted to work toward. The work was still there. My colleagues and business partners coped. Nothing broke.

After this incident, I was very aware of the fragility of my health. I became more intentional about spotting my triggers and symptoms. I prioritized my nutrition, hydration, fitness, and sleep. I scheduled breaks months ahead of when I needed them. I challenged behaviors related to perfectionism and indispensability. I also acknowledged that gratitude can coexist with dissatisfaction while finding joy in my work but doing what deeply mattered to me.

I was able to apply the learnings of this experience when my father died suddenly on January 23, 2019, and everything I knew to be true about life changed in an instant. His passing triggered this second incident of mental health struggle, but my symptoms differed.

Instead of insomnia, I could sleep for days on end. I cried all the time. I was highly anxious and unable to make simple decisions like which pair of jeans to wear, which made me cry more. I did not have suicidal thoughts exactly, but I remember hoping that the pain in my heart would take me away so I could see my dad again.

What was different on this occasion was that I immediately engaged the professional help of a psychiatrist and a therapist. They had a listening ear and the training to interpret what I didn't say. They recommended some helpful tools that placed me on the road to recovery much quicker than in my previous episodes. I didn't take extended time off work because it wasn't what I needed at the time. I needed human interaction so I didn't sink further into the darkness of my thoughts. Unfortunately, the finality of death means that I will never recover what I lost, but I learned to exist with the pain and eventually returned to productivity.

Now, it takes daily effort not to push myself to the limit, but I try to make the best choices for myself and my mental health.

MY ADVICE FOR YOU

The notable facts about my experiences are as follows:

- Very different events triggered them
- They came at different ages and stages of my life
- The severity and symptoms presented looked different each time
- They were largely unobserved by those closest to me because I could continue performing to a reasonably high standard. This proves that even the strongest, most high-performing people you know fight personal battles
- The solution was different each time

No one is exempt from challenges with their mind. I speak openly about my experience with burnout because I know that many suffer in silence. Here is some advice I would like to share with you on dealing with burnout.

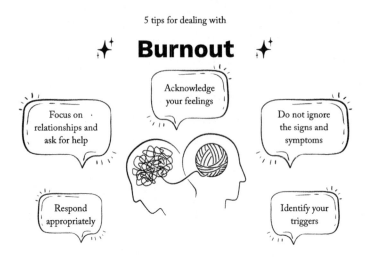

5 tips for dealing with

Burnout

Acknowledge your feelings

Focus on relationships and ask for help

Do not ignore the signs and symptoms

Respond appropriately

Identify your triggers

ACKNOWLEDGE THAT HOW YOU FEEL IS VALID

The world is constantly overheated. There is so much to do and so little time. Not only do we have to deal with our lives and manage our own emotions, we now have a front-row seat to other people's lives, issues, and feelings. This was also heightened during the COVID-19 pandemic when social media users noticed a boost in screen time. No wonder we are called the "anxious generation" (Marie, 2019). We are over-stimulated and over-exposed. If you feel stressed out, it's because this life is stressful. Give yourself a break.

DO NOT IGNORE THE SIGNS AND SYMPTOMS

How you feel is a very important yet usually ignored data point. What are your signs of burnout? Some common ones are exhaustion (which is different from being tired), reduced ability to focus on tasks, overeating or under-eating, crazy food cravings, headaches, muscle pain, physical shaking, slower exercise recovery times, disturbed sleep, anxiety, feeling overwhelmed, tearfulness, mood swings, and high emotional sensitivity (WebMD, 2022). Listen to your own body. It always cries out when something is amiss.

IDENTIFY YOUR BURNOUT TRIGGERS

These could be different every time. Below are some questions to ask yourself to discern what your burnout trigger is.

- Have you had any major life events such as births, deaths, new relationships, breakups, or illnesses in the family?
- Are there new demands or expectations on you, such as a new job, increased workload, or departure of help that you've relied upon?
- Are you adapting to new lifestyle changes, such as a new diet or exercise regime, financial changes, or a new commuting pattern?
- Have you come off an extraordinarily intense or happy season? Suppose you have spent months preparing for a wedding, your dream holiday, moving homes, or an exam. In that case, you may experience a slump when it is finally over. Recognize that while climbing a mountain is hard, coming down could pose different challenges.

RESPOND APPROPRIATELY

Once you can see the writing on the wall, reevaluate your priorities. Many things may be necessary, but not all things are a priority. Prioritization involves deciding which items on your to-do list can be eliminated, delayed, or delegated.

While addressing your to-do list is an excellent way of decompressing, the fact that something needs doing doesn't mean that it needs to be done by you. With several task management tools available like Fiverr, Task Rabbit, Otter ai, Deliveroo, and Bumble, to name a few, you can pretty much delegate anything. From cleaning, cooking, note-taking, editing, personal shopping, and even dating. Getting things done frees up your mental headspace, which can tremendously impact your mental well-being.

The next thing you should do is intentionally choose rest and enjoyment. Unfortunately, rest has been turned into a taboo word that reflects weakness, lack of drive, grit, or staying power. This is not true! When you go on a long drive, you stop at a service station to use the bathroom, get some food, take a nap, buy some fuel, or check that you are on the right path to your intended destination. Rest helps reduce the probability of cramping up, having an accident, or ending up in the wrong location.

Similarly, resting from the hustle and bustle of life and work is highly recommended to reenergize, unclutter, refuel, and recalibrate. Deciding to stop for rest does not mean you are giving up. It only means you are taking a break to recharge and return stronger.

If you find it challenging to rest, create systems that help you automate your rest and take the thinking and negotiating out of the process. For example, you may decide to take at least one day off in the week from work-related activities or plan your breaks well in advance of when you need to take them.

Take Uche Ezichi, an executive leadership coach, as an example. After suffering burnout in 2018, he adopted a practice of taking one day off work each week to "chill out and decompress." He also blocks out specific weeks every year to take off work. "I take these breaks around birthdays, anniversaries, and other sentimentally important events." Regardless of whatever Uche has going on, he blocks these dates off from the start of the year.

"I spend the time traveling and prioritizing my hobbies, like reading a good book or watching shows. I also dedicate time to thinking and doing other things that I enjoy, which is also a huge part of rest," Uche shared.

Having a regular pastime like reading, playing or watching sports, game night, going to the theatre, shopping, gardening, and many others, are essential to infusing joy and energy into your life.

Ultimately, the format and intensity of how people do or should respond to burnout are always different for each person and situation. Know that a right or wrong way to cope doesn't exist, but make sure that the result of whatever action you take is rejuvenation, a clearer headspace, and renewed energy. Like they say on airplanes, in an emergency, put on your oxygen mask before you try to help anyone else with theirs. Self-preservation is the name of the game.

FOCUS ON RELATIONSHIPS AND ASK FOR HELP

To reorganize your priorities and rest, you will need help. People don't read minds. Tell them what is going on so they can support you. You have nothing to be ashamed of!

- Ask your stakeholders (managers, clients, and colleagues) to take on some additional responsibilities and help you rebalance.
- Engage your support systems like your friends, family, and community.
- Seek professional help even if you feel you don't need it. Speak to your doctor, engage with a therapist, or call a crisis hotline. Think of this as the mental health version of taking an over-the-counter painkiller for a headache. Getting help is not taboo. Some employers have outsourced employee assistance programs that provide counseling, legal advice, and other services. Additionally, many organizations have in-house occupational health consultants who can help you navigate discussions with your managers about reducing your workload or taking time off. This is especially helpful if you don't have an organic support system like friends and family.

These are the steps I have on repeat as new stressors emerge in my own life, and I encourage you to do the same if you want to contribute value consistently. I am not a medical professional, so the advice given in this chapter should not be taken as medical advice. Instead, receive it as an appeal to pay attention to your physical and mental well-being so you can continue to be at your best.

YOUR TURN!

1. Pause for a few minutes to think about your physical health.
   - How would you rate the quality of your nutrition, hydration, exercise, and sleep?
   - If unsatisfied, write down some SMARTER health goals to help you get back on track.

2. Pause for a few minutes to think about your mental health.
   - Can you identify any of the symptoms mentioned in this chapter?
   - If yes, put the advised five-step action plan in motion.

PART 2

Summary: Contribute Value

HERE ARE SOME KEY TAKEAWAYS:

1. **Value is in the eye of the beholder.** If you want to be of value in any organization, you need to:
   - Identify your stakeholders—users, providers, governance, and influencers.
   - Understand their desires, problems, and goals.
   - Clarify and deliver solutions through your performance.
   - Elevate and improve your performance through up-skilling, diversifying your perspectives, taking risks, stretching yourself, and leveraging feedback.

2. **Avoiding bad behavior is as crucial as ensuring good performance.** Abide by the visible and invisible rules that govern acceptable behavior in your organization. Failure to do so can negatively impact perceptions of you and your career trajectory.

3. **You can always remedy mistakes.** If you have already made some mistakes, don't fret. You can fix the situation by acknowledging the error, apologizing where necessary, and taking steps to ensure that you no longer repeat your mistakes.

4. **Invest in building and fostering your network.** Networks are a set of connections and relationships made and maintained with the intention of achieving a mutually beneficial purpose or goal. They are pivotal for encouragement, advice, accountability, connection with others, resources, and opportunities.

5. **Leverage your network to deliver your best work.** A big part of delivering value lies in how well you can activate and optimize your personal, operational, and strategic networks to drive the results you want. At every stage of your career, you must ensure that your networks are valuable to and for you.

6. **Trust yourself.** Even where you perform well, behave well and have a great network. No one will trust you if you do not trust yourself. This trust is called confidence, the firm belief that you can create a successful outcome through your actions. This is the reason why people are willing to hire, promote, or pay you.

7. **Get ahead of fear and self-doubt.** Lack of confidence is typically the presence of self-doubt and is often a reflection of our fears and limiting beliefs. To deal with fears and limiting beliefs, apply the USER framework: understand them, identify their source, provide

alternative evidence to counter them, and replace or reframe your fears and beliefs with more empowering ones (DICE).

8. **Health is wealth.** Prioritize your physical and mental health so you remain in peak condition to deliver value sustainably.

PART 3

COMMUNICATE RESULTS

Work doesn't speak; people do.

Master the art of telling others the story of the work you do or have done, how you have done it, and why it is the solution to their most pressing problems. Being able to tell this story is the key to being recognized and adequately compensated. You cannot empower, influence, or rise to significance if you are not visible.

CHAPTER FOURTEEN

Market Yourself

"You cannot empower, influence, or rise to significance if you are not visible."

—*Mary Mosope Adeyemi*

****

Imagine this.

Every year, Apple Inc. engages thousands of people in countless hours of market research, imagination, design, innovation, and engineering to produce a suite of products that are highly coveted by a wide range of users. Imagine if they did this work only to lock these products in a warehouse, never to be seen or experienced by customers desperately needing them.

Would that make sense? I'm sure it would not.

Unfortunately, we do this when we do good work but shy away from sharing it.

According to CMO Survey, for-profit companies spend approximately 11–16 percent of their overall budget on marketing efforts for their products. This expense is even higher, at 30–40 percent, for companies in their infancy who invest more to build their brand and increase market awareness.

Similarly, you will have to spend time, effort, and money marketing your brand and results. This form of marketing is commonly called visibility: the art of demonstrating and communicating your value and the results you provide so that the right people can take notice.

Visibility is about being relevant in your industry or sphere of influence. You want to be identified as an individual and directly connected with the work that you do and the beliefs that you have.

As I shared before, the topic of visibility was a sticking point for me earlier in my career. I repeatedly got feedback that I needed to be more "visible," which I interpreted as "people need to see me more." I later learned that the visibility I sought was not only about being physically seen but, more importantly, adding value and then intentionally and repeatedly seeking ways to communicate the relevant results I was generating to those they matter to.

At the time, I was doing a halfhearted job at this. I was doing good work and producing results, but I expected my work to speak for itself. I didn't take any steps to share my work with my stakeholders. Like many capable professionals, I viewed the pursuit of visibility at work as bragging, self-promoting, and self-serving. But is it?

If you focus on creating value first, your pursuit of visibility will be less about you. Instead, it will be more about your work, how you have done it, and why it is the solution to the most pressing problems of your stakeholders. This is the story you need to master sharing. When you get value right, visibility is simply about packaging.

You have done the hard work. Now you need to shine the light on all you are and all you do.

THE IMPORTANCE OF VISIBILITY IN THE WORKPLACE

In his book *Empowering Yourself: The Organizational Game Revealed*, Harvey J. Coleman emphasizes the importance of visibility to career success in the Success PIE framework.

The premise of the framework is simple yet profound. Through his research, Coleman found that there are three essential elements needed to advance in your career: performance, image, and exposure.

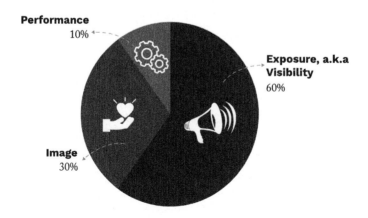

Performance
10%

Exposure, a.k.a Visibility
60%

Image
30%

- **Performance:** how good you are at your job and what outcomes you have delivered
- **Image:** how you are perceived
- **Exposure:** how well the right people know about you and what you do

More shocking and profound in his findings was the relative weight of these components of the success pie. Performance represented only 10 percent of the equation, image represented 30 percent, while exposure, a.k.a. visibility, represented a whopping 60 percent.

Just like I found out for myself, his message was simply this: while performance may be your entry ticket into the world of work, exposing your work to those who matter is what makes the difference. No one can exchange value with you if they are not even aware that you exist or that you are the solution to their problems.

Not being visible in your industry, company, department, or team can seriously impact your career trajectory. If your work is not visible, you are in danger of reducing your capacity to create value, creating a sponsorship gap, reducing your ability to influence others, or creating a representation or aspiration gap.

- When you **reduce your capacity to create value**, it doesn't matter how much good work you produce. Your good work only accrues value if others know it and it solves a problem for them.
- When you **create a sponsorship gap in your life**, you miss opportunities to increase your network, gain

promotion, earn more money, access innovative ideas, or participate in exciting and valuable projects.

- When you **reduce your ability to inspire, influence, and impact others**, you've missed how visibility creates a platform from which your work can spread beyond you. Visibility can also be a trigger that inspires others to recreate your success in their lives or learn from your mistakes. Remember that your story could be the one somebody has been waiting to read, and your voice could be the one somebody has been waiting to hear.
- When you **create a representation and aspiration gap** because you are not seen, your views and that of those you represent are not factored into decisions. You also inadvertently reduce the ability of others to aspire to the future you have accomplished.

CHIEF MARKETING OFFICER OF "PRODUCT YOU"

According to the CMO Survey, a chief marketing officer who drives the creation and implementation of marketing strategy is focused on three key areas: image and branding, advertising and promotion, and market intelligence and lead generation.

Likewise, focus your visibility efforts on these three areas. As CMO and chief storyteller of Product You, your job is to curate, advertise, and create opportunities for your brand.

01 IMAGE AND BRANDING   **02** ADVERTISING AND PROMOTION   **03** MARKET INTELLIGENCE AND LEAD GENERATION

IMAGE AND BRANDING

"Your brand is what other people say about you when you're not in the room."

—*Jeff Bezos*

What comes to mind when you hear these names: Oprah Winfrey, Richard Branson, Serena Williams, Steve Jobs, Elon Musk, and Rihanna Fenty? Of course, we identify these people by their names. But more importantly, these names trigger a thought or an emotion.

You may be thinking about the companies they lead and the value they create. You could also be thinking about their image, which includes their appearance, nationality, personality, mannerisms and vocal tone, values, and how they interact with the world. In any case, the collective impression you have about these and other people is called a brand.

- **Oprah Winfrey** is an African American talk show host, actress, author, and TV producer, as well as founder of Harpo Studios. She is known for her authenticity, generosity, and influence.
- **Richard Branson** is a British billionaire and founder of Virgin Group. He is known for his fun and adventurous persona.
- **Serena Williams** is an African American tennis champion and sister to Venus Williams. She is known for her boldness and sense of fashion and is committed to fighting racism and sexism on and off the court.
- **Steve Jobs** is the cofounder of Apple. He was often seen in a simple black turtleneck, a pair of jeans, and sneakers, and he was known for his innovation, grit, and determination.
- **Elon Musk** is an entrepreneur, inventor, and businessman. He is involved in Tesla, PayPal, SpaceX, and other innovative companies. He champions environmental consciousness and freedom of speech. He is known for his brilliance, audacity, and future-oriented focus.
- **Robyn "Rihanna" Fenty** is an award-winning musician from the Caribbean. She is the founder of Fenty Beauty and is known to be fashion-forward, eclectic, and sassy, with a strong mind for business.

When your name comes up, it should be recognized and trigger a recollection of one or more experiences upon which the perception of your value is based. Whether you are aware of it or not, you have a brand. People will always have an opinion of you, whether positive, negative, or neutral.

Your primary goal as CMO is to create that positive internal experience for your stakeholders when they think about you and to manage public perception through strategic storytelling. This intentional work creating and managing that perception is known as branding.

Taking a leaf from these well-known individuals, your brand should:

- **Be recognizable.** People should know your name when it is mentioned. This also translates to elements such as physical appearance and the clothes you typically wear. People may not use them as spoken descriptive details, but they form the mental image others have of you.
- **Represent the promises you make to your stakeholders.** Craft your brand around the strengths you want to emphasize in the workplace, like being thorough in your work or paying attention to detail.
- **Show off your authentic persona.** Your brand should be a genuine manifestation of who you are and should fit into your daily lifestyle. Otherwise, it will be challenging to keep up with it.
- **Communicate your values.** Use your brand to amplify what you believe in and care about, which won't be too hard if you know what matters to you. For example, although I am a credit risk manager, I am also known for the work I do in people development as well as gender and racial diversity because these are topics that I deeply care about. Consequently, I am often asked to join diversity councils and speak on panels related to these topics.

- **Be worthy of value exchange.** Those that engage with your brand should be able to conceptualize what they are getting from you in exchange for their investment in you.

ADVERTISING AND PROMOTION

To advertise or promote means to call the public's attention to your product or service.

—*Oxford Dictionary*

The individuals mentioned above became household names because they were intentional about marketing themselves alongside the work they do. Some of them—like Oprah, who regularly films herself cooking, reading, or having conversations—opened their lives and homes to us. Some—like Richard Branson, who uses platforms like LinkedIn as an outlet for his thought leadership—interact with the public on social media. And some—like Elon Musk, who decided he would start The Boring Company on Twitter because he was stuck in traffic—let us into what they are thinking or plan to do next. Like Serena Williams—who is open about the plight of women and people of color in sports and other areas, which has led her to start her investment platform, Serena Ventures, to invest in founders from underrepresented backgrounds—they even share their passions, inspiration, and problems with us. All of this communicates their brand to us.

As CMO, actively discuss your work and the results you are getting, showcase your knowledge and expertise, and share your brand story. Here are a few ways you can do this:

TELL PEOPLE WHAT YOU DO

One thing always surprises me when I interact with young professionals. They often say that visibility is one of their top career challenges, yet when I ask them if or how they share their work, I get awkward silence and blank stares.

While it may seem obvious, your role as CMO is to tell your stakeholders, "Hey, I'm here, and this is why you should care." Regularly share these four things when talking about the work that you have done:

- What you have done
- Why you have done it
- How you have done it
- How it is the solution to their most desperate problem

SHARE YOUR KNOWLEDGE

Sharing your knowledge is an effective way of showcasing your expertise on a particular subject. You can do this both internally and externally. You can train your colleagues at work, speak at an industry conference or as a guest on a podcast, and write articles on LinkedIn or on your blog on a subject of interest.

Regardless of how small or large the stage is, this is an excellent one-to-many strategy that will exponentially improve your visibility.

SHARE YOUR STORY

People are not just interested in the story of your work output but also the story of the process. They want to know the good decisions you made and the lessons learned along the way.

Knowing this helps you weave your work story into your life story, and it allows others to connect with you more deeply as they find common ground with one or more parts of who you are.

A variety of opportunities for advertising and promotion are available to you. You can promote yourself by telling your story in one-on-one conversations, online meetings, conferences, networking events, and on social media.

Anywhere you can connect with people (see Chapter Ten) is a platform on which you can tell others what you do and share your knowledge and story.

MARKET INTELLIGENCE AND LEAD GENERATION

This function is a more strategic rather than an operational one. As CMO, invest time in understanding how the industry landscape and the broader world of work are changing and what opportunities those changes may present for you.

In executing this, you must stay abreast of industry trends, connect with people beyond what you need (see strategic networks in Chapter Ten), and look around corners to see what may be coming your way. Some practical ways of doing this from your current seat are leveraging community and collaborating with others.

LEVERAGE COMMUNITY

Joining affinity and shared interest groups where you can network with like-minded people is a great way to gather information on what is coming down the pipeline in that space.

COLLABORATE WITH OTHERS

Leverage your mentors, sponsors, and peer coaches to help you look beyond your current seat and position yourself as someone open to new and exciting things.

Seun Toye-Kayode is a strategic program lead at a global investment firm. Seun and I spoke about how utilizing her strengths, adding value, and visibility drove her to get and thrive in a senior role only seven years into her career.

"The opportunity came from my work with affinity networks, particularly our firm-wide Black and women's networks," she said. One of Seun's sponsors allowed her to moderate a discussion on diversity and inclusion with the European CEO as part of the firm's International Women's Day programming.

"This moved the dial for me because it put me on the radar of other partners at the firm. People could see that I am naturally good at having conversations, communicating complex problems, and laying out a vision that people can rally around. I could leverage those skills in the workplace. From then on, every other month, I was asked to speak on some panel or moderate a conversation, giving me even more visibility in the firm and with key senior stakeholders." This ended up being the reason Seun stood out in interviews, landing her in a senior role.

Intentional visibility has continued to serve Seun in her role as she continues communicating the results she produces for the firm.

"I organized a tour to meet with some of the founders we support across Europe. When I returned, I emailed senior stakeholders to post them on what we had done and how we added value," she said.

Seun also shared emails from founders who attended the tour programming regarding how they felt about the firm's commitment to them. This was well received by her senior leaders. "I received overwhelmingly positive feedback around the impact I was making, how it is brand accretive for the firm, and how it's helping the firm build a strong reputation around a key strategic objective. Some partners also forwarded my email to the firm's CEO."

As Seun reflected on the moment, she said, "What was so powerful for me was that my role is something that I am passionate about. So, to see the value it was adding and see it so deeply appreciated was very satisfying. It was also a reminder that I have to ensure I continue to do work that puts me in the position to feel this way about myself and not just about the quality of work produced."

There are many things Seun's experience highlights for me, and hopefully for you too:

- Leading with value is critically important in your pursuit of visibility.
- Sharing your knowledge and story plays a key role in gaining exponential visibility.
- Crafting your career around your strengths and authentic brand can make your work more enjoyable and satisfying.
- Your network or communities can play an influential role in market intelligence and lead generation in your career.

- Visibility can have a ripple effect on your ability to access opportunities and be successful in them.

YOUR TURN!

1. Consider your brand.
    - What three words describe the experience other people have of you when they interact with you?
    - What three words describe how you want to be perceived in the workplace?
    - If there is a disconnect, think about how you can close the gap.

CHAPTER FIFTEEN
Be Visibly Valuable

"Visibility without value is vanity."

—*Bernard Kelvin Clive*

****

When you enter a dark room, the first thing you do is reach for the light switch. This reaction is natural. After all, who wants to stumble around in the dark? The same principle applies when it comes to visibility in the workplace.

In a competitive workplace, taking every opportunity to increase your visibility is essential. That means you must proactively seek opportunities to showcase your skills and capabilities. However, you can easily get caught up in the daily grind and forget about visibility altogether. That's why it's crucial to have clear, readily implementable visibility strategies.

By developing a visibility plan, you ensure that you consistently put your best foot forward and drive awareness for your brand.

STRATEGIES FOR VALUE-LED
VISIBILITY IN THE WORKPLACE

Whether volunteering for high-profile projects, taking on additional responsibilities outside of your comfort zone, sharing your thought leadership, or being active on social media, proactively putting yourself in the spotlight will help you stand out among your colleagues.

I have applied and would like to suggest a few practical strategies you can implement to increase your visibility in the workplace. Each of them aims to showcase your valuable contribution to as many people as possible.

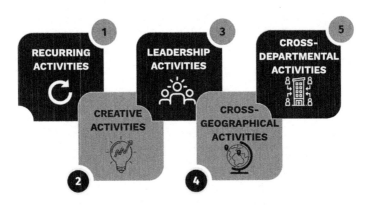

RECURRING ACTIVITIES

Perform an action that needs to be executed regularly with high frequency. Ideally, this is something you can take ownership of and in which you can become an expert. This demonstrates your ability to stay consistent, be responsible, and own a process. It also gives you name recognition.

Some examples of this include:

- Send out weekly market or product updates
- Share summary achievements (e.g., deal summaries, P&L updates, etc.) to your team, department, and other stakeholders
- Coordinate the agenda for regular team meetings
- Plan quarterly social events

As an associate, I volunteered to manage the "deals in syndication" process. Every week, I asked my colleagues in capital markets to provide an update on how the transactions we had in the market were performing. Following this, I shared my notes with senior risk officers keen to receive updates on how the firm was actively reducing our loan exposure.

Mine was a middleman role that only required me to gather and synthesize information. However, I added significant value to my stakeholders. The information I provided saved them time and aided quick decision-making. I acted as the contact for teams involved with syndicating loan positions in and outside the risk department. People identified my name with the task I performed and through which I added value. They trusted the quality of my work and my consistency.

Within weeks of serving in this capacity, I got a call from our chief risk officer asking me to clarify one of the data points on my report. Thankfully, I was able to provide him with the information he needed. He was so senior in the organization that I would ordinarily not have access to him.

I also learned about various transactions, financing structures, and capital markets, and expanded my operational network within the firm due to my exposure. These would not have been possible if I was not executing this weekly action.

CREATIVE ACTIVITIES

Perform an action that demonstrates your creativity. You can start, stop, enhance, or change something critical to management's strategy for the year. You could also fix a product, process, or people issue that bothers you or others.

Some examples of this include:

- Join a new product, process, or system launch team
- Identify existing processes that you can improve to achieve efficiencies or other KPIs
- Codify a regular activity into a policy, procedure, or guideline

Over the course of a few months, my team once received several lending requests for infrastructure-style financing for telecommunication companies. We hadn't executed this financing format very frequently in the firm, so we had no policy to guide consistent underwriting practices. When we closed a few of these transactions, I decided to create some guidelines. It took a few weeks of analysis and discussion with business partners and risk leaders to develop standards that all stakeholders supported.

This was of immense value to my stakeholders because we could meet regulatory expectations to have underwriting standards for material businesses. It also helped my team better advise our business partners and make quicker decisions on client requests.

This was an opportunity to demonstrate my creativity, out-of-the-box thinking, presentation skills, and management of stakeholders across the firm, which increased my visibility.

LEADERSHIP ACTIVITIES

Stretch yourself by taking on a leadership role. You don't need to be the one coming up with ideas, but you can demonstrate your ability to execute, lead, and drive change. Some examples of this include:

- Regularly update stakeholders on noteworthy developments.
- Provide critical strategic direction and motivation for a team of people on a project.

I once volunteered to lead a project to develop a new framework and process for reviewing client performance. I am a subject matter expert, and I enjoy process development and project management, so I knew that I would be able to apply my strengths to execute this task successfully.

I set up my strategic and operational project plans and presented them to the operating committee for approval. This committee included the head of credit risk and about ten global industry leads to whom I typically wouldn't have access.

After securing the green light to proceed, I recruited my project team and began working.

A few weeks later, we had the process up and running. The first review meeting was held virtually with over a hundred global credit risk professionals, including some senior leaders. I had the opportunity to present the work my team and I had done, the regulatory expectations we were working to meet, and what we expected from the group each quarter.

After making some opening remarks on the state of the market, I handed the presentation off to each industry team to present their reviews of the client. In one meeting, our global team knew my name, saw my face, and experienced my capabilities.

Every quarter, when it was time for this review, I had to interact with several stakeholders to verify data, prepare talking points, sync calendars, and document the meeting minutes. My work was valuable because I supported our department in satisfying a regulatory requirement. I also helped our global team coordinate what would otherwise be a very complicated and disjointed process.

My success with this activity earned me an invitation to join the operating committee. I went from presenting to this group to being part of them. The experience was an excellent opportunity to create and lead a recurring action, a fantastic culmination of the three strategies we have covered.

CROSS-GEOGRAPHICAL ACTIVITIES

Work on a project with colleagues in a different geographic location than yours. The benefits of doing this are that it demonstrates your ability to collaborate and strengthens your relationship with global colleagues. It also opens you to geographical mobility opportunities and access to international leaders.

Some examples of this include:

- Participate in global initiatives like recruitment and training.
- Join an international product, process, or system team.
- Participate in a regulatory change project that impacts multiple regions.

While at BoA, I joined the global policy review team that led the process of reviewing each of our policies every year. The team comprised credit risk colleagues of different seniority levels across our primary business geographies: the Americas, Europe, the Middle East, and Asia-Pacific.

Our work was valuable because it was part of our annual regulatory compliance process. For about a month, this group met for two hours daily to discuss proposed policy changes. I enjoyed hearing how regional differences influenced our perspectives on how policies could be enhanced and applied.

Where we recommended changes to the policy, this group presented those changes to the global risk team, which meant more eyes on my work and exponential growth for my visibility. Participating in this activity allowed me to demonstrate critical thinking, subject matter expertise, analytical rigor, and attention to detail to a group of global colleagues I did not work with on a daily basis.

CROSS-DEPARTMENTAL ACTIVITIES

Work on a project with colleagues in a different department than yours. The benefits of doing this are that it demonstrates your ability to collaborate, builds your operational network, opens you up to internal mobility opportunities, offers access to other senior leaders, and allows for exposure to other departments and how they fit into the bigger picture.

Some examples of this include:

- Participating in firm-wide recruitment, mentoring, and mobility programs.
- Becoming a member of an affinity network where those with shared interests or demography come together to support each other.

A few years ago, while at BoA, some of my global colleagues who identify as African came together to create the Africa Program. The program was a cross-departmental recruitment initiative to hire junior talent from universities in Nigeria and Ghana to our office in the United Kingdom. This recruitment initiative was the first of its kind in the UK office, and I was thrilled to be part of the team spearheading the cause. The program was valuable as one of our firm's diversity recruitment initiatives, and we knew the positive impact it could have on a young person's career.

The project team had multiple meetings with departmental heads to pitch the program. Some signed up, and others did not. We had to pitch to our CFO to secure the budget covering the expenses. We also had to connect with the universities we wanted to pilot the program. We then recruited colleagues across the firm to support the training and mentoring of the students.

My visibility across the firm skyrocketed as a result of my involvement. I met many senior leaders and colleagues in other departments passionate about leveling the playing field for underrepresented talent. Many of these people are still very close friends. Over the years, this program expanded to include new departments and geographies, which allowed me to interact with and showcase my capabilities to more people.

You can apply these strategies at any stage of your career to increase your visibility in the workplace and position yourself for success.

VIRTUAL VISIBILITY

As we wrap up this discussion on visibility, I want to highlight some additional actions you can take to stand out in an increasingly virtual workplace.

1. **Participate** in virtual team meetings, town halls, and industry events. Ask questions, share what you are working on, provide feedback, and present information.
2. **Video over voice** is key. Research shows that you significantly reduce your impact in virtual meetings by

turning off your video. Prioritize turning your video on to emphasize your presence and engagement.

3. **Share your work** with your manager daily or in weekly summaries since they naturally have less visibility of your work in a virtual arrangement. You can also share materials your team and business partners will find helpful, such as articles and market updates. Leverage social media to connect with others and share stories of the work you are doing and the lessons you learn along the way.

4. **Catch up with people** and maintain regular one-on-one meetings with your manager, coworkers, and industry colleagues.

5. **Collaborate** and prioritize team-based contribution over individual contribution. This way, you have more eyes on your work and can leverage other people's platforms to increase your visibility.

6. **Social events** are your friend. Attend even the virtual ones. Some teams host games nights, virtual drinks, and other fun events online so that the team continues to foster relationships that help them deliver better together.

YOUR TURN!

1. Think about the strategies for value-led visibility.
   - What opportunities do you see around you to implement these?

Summary: Communicate Results

HERE ARE SOME KEY TAKEAWAYS:

1. **Visibility is not just about being seen**. Being visible is the art of demonstrating and communicating your value and the results you provide so that the right people can take notice and exchange value for value.

2. **You are the chief marketing officer of Product You**. Consequently, your job is to create and manage your brand and be its chief storyteller.

3. **Visibility is the packaging for the value you have delivered**. You can improve your visibility in any sphere by being a person of value, intentionally telling people what you do, sharing your knowledge and your story, leveraging community, and collaborating with others.

4. **Visibility doesn't happen without a strategy**. Find the value-led visibility strategy that works for you and be intentional about making a great impression.

5. **Virtual visibility is a must**. As our workplaces become more virtual, make sure you participate actively in virtual rooms, leverage social media to share your work, prioritize catching up with others as well as collaborative projects, and attend social events with your colleagues.

Continue the Cycle

"In order to keep up with the world of 2050, you will need not merely to invent new ideas and products but above all to reinvent yourself again and again."

—*Yuval Noah Harari*

****

Do you believe in chance and luck, or cause and effect?

I believe in both.

Yes, events in your life could be a product of random circumstances beyond your control. For example, you could have been born into a wealthy or poverty-stricken family simply by chance. However, I also believe that you have the power to create your luck. Every action has a consequence, and every decision leads to a specific outcome. What you may consider chance or luck is often the benefit of someone else's action or inaction. In other words, every event is determined by a series of prior events and results from cause and effect.

In the workplace, both chance and luck as well as cause and effect are at work. You can't control the former, so why not focus on the latter? Make your own luck. Make yourself visible.

In your *Visible Strengths* three-part journey, we looked at a strategy for ensuring your value doesn't go unnoticed.

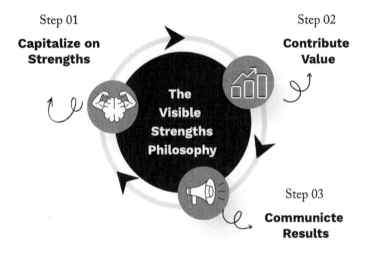

Step 01

Capitalize on Strengths

Step 02

Contribute Value

The Visible Strengths Philosophy

Step 03

Communicte Results

How to capitalize on your strengths: You learned the importance of a strengths-based approach in your career. You discovered your strengths from inside and outside, clarified what matters to you, and created SMARTER career goals supported by effective strategy. All of these helped you figure out how you will intentionally craft the career of your dreams around your strengths.

How to contribute value: You learned that value is in the eye of the beholder, so understanding who your stakeholders are and what they need from you is paramount to being valuable. You identified your stakeholders and prioritized their needs. You also learned to contribute value through your innovative performance, operating principles, and supportive network. You focused on how to prioritize your physical and mental health on the journey so you can give value consistently.

How to communicate your results: You learned that visibility drives a significant part of our success metrics at work. However, that visibility is not just about being physically seen but about adding value, intentionally and repeatedly seeking ways to communicate relevant results to those they matter to. Your role as CMO of Product You cannot be overestimated as you create your brand, advertise it, and create new opportunities for it in the ever-changing world of work.

So, if you are asking, "What next?" I say, *repeat*!

This is the very essence of the Visible Strengths Philosophy.

As you apply your strengths to contribute value and then communicate your results, more opportunities will open up for you to use your strengths, contribute more value, and communicate more results. It's a never-ending cycle because you will always have an opportunity to elevate and redefine your thresholds of success.

With many possible twists and turns in your career, agility is an increasingly important skill needed to future-proof your career. At any stage of your career, in any industry and in any seat you occupy, fulfillment and success in your career will always boil down to these three elements, which you can apply as narrowly or as widely as you need to.

The Visible Strengths Philosophy is the springboard you use to scale through challenging situations in the workplace. It gives you the confidence to work with and through a difficult client or project. It helps you make an indisputable case for a promotion or pay raise. You rely on it when exploring new career opportunities in the same field or a new one. Focusing on your strengths, value, and visible results will boost your tenacity.

The Visible Strengths Philosophy is the drawing board you go back to when you face inevitable setbacks in your career and need the wisdom and energy to bounce back. When you don't get the job or the promotion, your contract is not renewed, or your role is made redundant, you suffer a dip in your passion or get bored. Focusing on your strengths, value, and visible results will boost your resilience.

Ultimately, the role models who achieve the career heights to which so many aspire are where they are today because they continued this cycle. Even when the going got tough, they took the time they needed to heal their wounds, reconnect with their value proposition, and return to the battlefield to continue adding value every day in new and innovative ways.

As you continue your cycle, you will be more efficient in applying each element and transitioning between steps. Your muscles will keep getting stronger because you put them to good use.

As we wrap up, I want to ask you again those three questions we began with.

1. Is your work crafted around your natural gifts and talents?

2. Can you use those talents to solve problems for the people and organizations you serve?
3. Do the relevant people know that you exist and are worthy of their attention and sponsorship?

If you have engaged with this book fully by reading the chapters and doing the exercises, I trust you feel more empowered to answer these questions with a resounding *Yes*, *Yes*, and *Yes*.

I hope you have clarity on your path, confidence in your choices, and the courage to define your success for yourself and step into what you want to achieve in life. Continue to capitalize on strengths, contribute value, communicate results, and repeat!

YOUR TURN!
I promised you that at the end of this book, we would return to these exercises from Chapter One and celebrate your transformation.

1. Project: Think about a recent project you worked on. How did you apply the three elements of the Visible Strengths Philosophy?
   – I capitalized on my strengths by:
   – I contributed value by doing:
   – I communicated the following results:

2. Career: Reflect on your current job. How are you applying the three elements of the Visible Strengths Philosophy?
   – I am capitalizing on my strengths by:
   – I am contributing value by doing:
   – I am communicating my results by:

Acknowledgments

"When eating fruit, remember the one who planted the tree."
— *Vietnamese Proverb*

****

This book in your hands would not have been possible without the inspiration, love, and support of the many people I am blessed to call family, friends, colleagues, mentors, mentees, and students. Some planted the tree and others watered it, and now many will eat its fruit. Thank you so much!

First, to God Almighty, the giver of all knowledge, wisdom, and understanding. In you, I live, I move, and have my being. Thank you for honoring me with good gifts that make me rich and add no sorrow. Thank you for holding me in your hands through this journey. Thank you for filling me with clarity, confidence, and courage so I can now sow those seeds in others. I am humbled by this mandate that is *Visible Strengths*, and I will endeavor to bring you alone all the glory.

To my mother, Chief Elizabeth Omotayo Adeyemi. Your dedication to people, work ethic, and consistency shine on my path. Thank you for always being my champion and showing me how proud you are of me. Thank you for being relentless in your prayers for me. Those prayers have held me up as I have birthed this book amidst various challenges.

To my family and friends, thank you for your constant calls with words of encouragement and empowerment through the past twelve months. I am grateful.

To those who have impacted me significantly by sharing their stories with me:

- Anna-Noémie Ouattara Boni
- Busola Banjo
- Bukola Adisa
- Damilola Fajuyigbe
- Deborah Ajaja
- Mojolaoluwa Aderemi-Makinde
- Kike Sanyaolu
- Oluchi Ikechi
- Rolake Akinkugbe Filani
- Sabrina Francis
- Seun Toye-Kayode
- Uche Ezichi
- Students of the Visible Strengths Program

Your generosity and vulnerability are why I could string these words and chapters together. Thank you for trusting me to share your inspirational career stories to inspire and equip others.

Invaluable to me over the years are a few sources of inspiration who have significantly influenced the content of this book:

- Bozoma Saint John, veteran CEO
- Dara Treasdar, Head of Global Marketing and Communications at Peloton
- Dr. Ola Brown, founder of Flying Doctors Healthcare Investment Company
- Helen Tupper and Sarah Ellis, authors of *The Squiggly Career* and *You Coach You*
- Kathy Kay and Claire Shipman, authors of *The Confidence Code*
- Kike Oniwinde, founder of BYP Network
- May Busch, executive coach
- Michelle Obama, former First Lady of the United States of America and author of *Becoming*
- Rosalind Brewer, CEO of Walgreens Boots Alliance
- Sheryl Sandberg, ex-COO of Meta and author of *Lean In: Women, Work, and the Will to Lead*
- Sylvana Caloni, leadership coach and ex-president of the Women in Banking and Finance network
- Thasunda Brown Duckett, CEO of Teachers Insurance and Annuity Association of America
- Whitney Wolfe Herd, founder and CEO of Bumble

Thank you! Your work and stories have been helpful and inspiring to me, and I hope to many others as well.

To the team at Creator Institute and New Degree Press, thank you for providing a platform to bring my book to life:

- To Professor Eric Koester, I came into this process with so much doubt (I know! The irony of it all), but with each conversation, you opened my eyes to the possibility that I, too, could become an author.
- To my development editor, Karina Agbist, thank you for always having a calm disposition, a listening ear, and an encouraging voice. Each time we spoke, you met my ideas with enthusiasm, which gave me the courage to carry on.
- To my marketing revisions editor, Faiqa Zafar, you said we would get through this, and we did. Thank you for helping me get out of my head and helping me connect the dots. You kept pushing me forward even when I wanted to run and hide. I am so grateful.
- To the rest of this incredible team—Brian Bies, Kyra Ann Dawkins, John Saunders, Hayley Newlin, Hannah Enriquez, Natalie Bailey, Asia Mcdougall, Linda Berardelli, Heather Gomez, Nikolina Sivački, Amanda Brown, and Gjorgji Pejkovski—thank you for all you have sowed into me in this process.

To the *Visible Strengths* author community, you are my 107 blessings and I am honored to name you in this book! Thank you for investing in my author journey, advocating for me, reading good and mediocre drafts, and giving your input along the way. I demanded so much of you, and you delivered with excellence. I am so very thankful to and for you.

In alphabetical order by first or company name:

Abdul Nasir
Ajoke Tella
Aman Ahluwalia
Amuche Ekemezie
Anna-Noémie Ouattara Boni
Arit Udoh
Audrey Ampofo
Ayodele Ofi
Bayo Adelaja
(and Do It Now Now Ltd)
Bayo Adeyemi
Beatrice Lawale
Bukola Adisa (and Career
Masterclass Limited)
Bukunmi Adeyemi
Chi-chi Etiaba
Chisom Eyesan
Dami Banjo
Daniella Sterling
Dara Osinubi
Debo Fletcher
Deborah Ajaja
Donatila Smajli
Efemena Yugbovwre
Elizabeth Isola
Eloho Efemuai
Esther Olaleye
Evangel Monima-Harrison
Femi Adeyemi
Feyi Adegbohun
Fola Akinbayo
Fola Oyeleye

Folakemi Sebiotimo
Folasayo Williams
Genevieve Opara
Ginika Amanerimi
Goziam Okogwu
Grace Adewale
Gwendolyne Brown
Hannah Opoku
Janet Ore
Jeffrey Bryant
Jessica Sugru Ali
Jire Ogunsanya
Jola Aderemi-Makinde
Joys Alabi
Kachi Tila-Adesina
Kamaru Alofoje
Kemi Adetu
Kene Onyeka Allison
Kikelomo Sanyaolu
Lade Ayediran
Lamide Akinwuntan
Lara Talabi
Lara Tijani
McKinsey & Company
Mariam Saraki
Mariolla Asare
Mariza Morris
Mary Fafemi
Michael Olugbo Adeyemi
Moriam Odunayo Balogun
Nicole Morgan
Nifemi Aluko

Nneka Diobi
Nogie Oguwa
Odunayo Oyelese
Oghenevona Ezichi
Olamide Fafemi
Olamidotun Votu-Obada
Oler Oler
Oloruntobi Erinoso
Oludamilola Akinbayo
Olukoleayo Majekodunmi
Oluwadara Odejide
Oluwakemi Atilola
Oyewunmi Rotimi
Oyinkansola Adebayo
(and Niyo Enterprise)
Ozaze Osoba
Pearle Amobi
Rabia khans
Remi Babalola
Remilekun Olowu
Renee Sterling
Rotimi Adeyemi
Rume Ameke
Salimat Abdullahi

Shalom Usman
Sheri Bello-Osagie
Sophia Dery
Stephanie Apokhume
Steve Ohene
Tanaka Dube
Tayo Fashina
Timi Adelaja
Titi Oliyide
Tokunboh Akinlonu
Tomi Ibirogba
Toyin Oboh
Toyin Oduyemi
Tracey Abayeta
(and Lazard Bank)
Uche Ezichi
Vese Aghoghovbia
Victoria Adeyemi
Victoria Enoc-Ahiamadu
Vome Aghoghovbia-Gafaar
Yemisi Akinbayo
Yemisi Olaleye
Yeside Odumade

And to *you*, the real heroes of this story! You made a commitment to your career by picking up this book. I hope it paid off.

Thank you for trusting me with your precious time and your physical or virtual bookshelf space. Thank you for the honor of letting my voice influence your career, business, and hopefully your life journey. I do not take that privilege for granted.

This book almost didn't happen, but I kept thinking about you. Thank you for keeping me accountable to obey God's call on my life.

This book is my love letter to you. I hope you read it well, grow, and share it with others.

Bibliography

INTRODUCTION

Barth, Diane. "Success is a process, not an achievement." *Quartz at Work* (blog), November 12, 2018. https://qz.com/work/1460466/am-i-successful/.

Deloitte. "The Deloitte Global 2022 Gen Z & Millennial Survey." Accessed May 19, 2022. https://www2.deloitte.com/content/dam/Deloitte/global/Documents/deloitte-2022-genz-millennial-survey.pdf.

Gallup. "How to Improve My Career: 02 What Career is Right for Me?" *CliftonStrengths*. Accessed January 5, 2022. https://www.gallup.com/cliftonstrengths/en/299855/how-to-improve-my-career.aspx#ite-304610.

Henley Business School. "How 'woke' is the future of work?" September 12, 2019. https://www.henley.ac.uk/news/2019/how-woke-is-the-future-of-work.

CHAPTER TWO

Bartlett, Steven (@stevenbartlett). "And that's episode 1 done!" LinkedIn, January 7, 2022. Video, 5:25. https://www.linkedin.com/posts/stevenbartlett-123_and-thats-episode-1-done-honestly-activity-6885132181782446080-Mux8/.

Brown, Ola. "My journey from medical doctor to pan-African healthcare investor." *Medium* (blog). November 19, 2020. https://medium.com/@drola/my-journey-from-medical-doctor-to-pan-african-healthcare-investor-d740488cd15.

Brown, Ola. "The Flying Doctors Healthcare Investment Company at 10!" *Medium* (blog). March 21, 2020. https://medium.com/@drola/the-flying-doctors-healthcare-investment-company-at-10-dc1ff6c927a3.

Buckingham, Marcus. "Know Your Strengths, Own Your Strengths." *Lean In*. Video, 18.15. Accessed January 22, 2022.

https://leanin.org/education/know-your-strengths-own-your-strengths-no-one-else-will.

Busch, May. "3 Essential Areas to Focus on for Career Success in 2022." *May Busch Creating Leaders* (blog). Accessed January 10, 2022. https://maybusch.com/3-essential-areas-focus-career-success-2022/.

Cherry, Kendra. "What Is the Negativity Bias?" *Verywellmind* (blog). April 29, 2020. https://www.verywellmind.com/negative-bias-4589618.

Gallup. "Learn About the Science of CliftonStrengths." Accessed January 10, 2022. https://www.gallup.com/cliftonstrengths/en/253790/science-of-cliftonstrengths.aspx.

The Flying Doctors Healthcare Investment Company. "Portfolio." Accessed January 10, 2022. https://fdhic.com/portfolio/.

The Flying Doctors Healthcare Investment Company. "The FDHIC Catalyst Fund." Accessed January 10, 2022. https://fdhic.com/fdhic-catalyst-fund/.

Tupper, Helen, and Sarah Ellis. *The Squiggly Career*. United Kingdom: Penguin Random House UK, 2019.

CHAPTER THREE

16Personalities. "Free Personality Test." Accessed January 20, 2022. https://www.16personalities.com/free-personality-test.

Evans, Mary Claire, and Adam Hickman. "How CliftonStrengths Compares with Insights Discovery?" *Gallup: CliftonStrengths*. March 11, 2019. https://www.gallup.com/cliftonstrengths/en/249434/compare-insights-discovery-cliftonstrengths.aspx.

Evans, Mary Claire, and Adam Hickman. "How Do CliftonStrengths and the VIA Survey Compare?" *Gallup: CliftonStrengths*. March 17, 2021. https://www.gallup.com/cliftonstrengths/en/249878/compare-via-survey-cliftonstrengths.aspx.

Hickman, Adam. "How Do CliftonStrengths and MBTI (Myers-Briggs) Compare?" *Gallup: CliftonStrengths*, February 2, 2021. https://www.gallup.com/cliftonstrengths/en/250133/compare-mbti-myers-briggs-cliftonstrengths.aspx.

CHAPTER FOUR

BYP Network. "Our Values." June 4, 2020. https://byp.network/values/.

Cision PR Newswire. "TIAA Appoints Thasunda Brown Duckett President and CEO." Cision PR Newswire news release, February 25, 2021, on the Cision PR Newswire website, accessed January 21, 2022.

https://www.prnewswire.com/news-releases/tiaa-appoints-thasunda-brown-duckett-president-and-ceo-301235787.html.

Connley, Courtney. "Why Thasunda Brown Duckett, TIAA's next CEO, accepted her lowest job offer after college." *CNBC: Make It.* March 1, 2021. Accessed January 21, 2022.
https://www.cnbc.com/2021/03/01/tiaa-ceo-thasunda-brown-duckett-on-accepting-lowest-job-offer-after-college.html.

Corsetti, Cynthia. "What I Learned from *Howard's Gift*." Accessed May 22, 2022.
https://www.cynthiacorsetti.com/book-review-howards-gift/.

Smith, Maggie (@maggiesmithpoet). "Even if you don't believe you have 'a purpose,' think about the work you can do in the world that would make a difference to others. What art can you make, what comfort can you bring, what wrong can you set right? If you can do it, you should do it. Keep moving." Twitter, July 3, 2020, 12:54 p.m.
https://twitter.com/maggiesmithpoet/status/1279020601819226112.

The New York Times. "Thasunda Brown Duckett of Chase: People Need to Know Who You Are." Accessed January 21, 2022.
https://www.nytimes.com/2019/04/04/business/thasunda-duckett-jpmorgan-corner-office.html.

Thrash, Todd M. and Andrew J. Elliot. "Inspiration as a Psychological Construct." *Journal of Personality and Social Psychology* 84, no. 4 (May 2003): 871–89. 10.1037/0022-514.84.4.871.
https://www.researchgate.net/publication/10796715_Inspiration_as_a_Psychological_Construct.

Tony Robbins. "What are Values?" Accessed January 21, 2022.
https://www.tonyrobbins.com/mind-meaning/our-set-of-rules/.

Tupper, Helen, and Sarah Ellis. *You Coach You.* United Kingdom: Penguin Random House UK, 2022

Wakefield, Jane. "The tech billionaire who is putting women first." *BBC News.* April 7, 2021.
https://www.bbc.co.uk/news/technology-56662100.

CHAPTER FIVE

Haughey, Duncan. "A Brief History of SMART Goals." ProjectSmart, Dec 13, 2014. Accessed January 10, 2022.
https://www.projectsmart.co.uk/smart-goals/brief-history-of-smart-goals.php.

Locke, Edwin A. and Gary P. Latham. "New Directions in Goal-Setting Theory," *Current Directions in Psychological Science* 15, no. 5 (October 2006): 265–268.
https://doi.org/10.1111/j.1467-8721.2006.00449.x.

Matthews, Gail. "Goals Research Summary." Accessed September 30, 2021.
https://www.dominican.edu/sites/default/files/2020-02/gailmatthews-harvard-goals-researchsummary.pdf.

Murphy, Mark. "Neuroscience Explains Why You Need to Write Down Your Goals If You Actually Want to Achieve Them." *Forbes*, April 15, 2018. https://www.forbes.com/sites/markmurphy/2018/04/15/neuroscience-explains-why-you-need-to-write-down-your-goals-if-you-actually-want-to-achieve-them/.

Rao, Paulette. "The Role of Commitment and Motivation in Goal Achievement." August 11, 2019. https://www.linkedin.com/pulse/role-commitment-motivation-goal-achievement-paulette-rao-mcc-bcc/.

Stanford Graduate School of Business. "Sheryl Sandberg, COO of Facebook, on Using Your Voice for Good." June 1, 2017. Video, 49:20. https://www.gsb.stanford.edu/insights/sheryl-sandberg-careers-arent-ladders-theyre-jungle-gyms.

CHAPTER SIX

Dreamstime. "Ikigai, meaning of life concept." Accessed May 29, 2022. https://www.dreamstime.com/stock-illustration-ikigai-meaning-life-concept-vector-illustration-self-realisation-minimalistic-style-image67962160.

Gallup. "Create a Culture That Inspires: Name, Claim, Aim Strengths." *CliftonStrengths*. June 18, 2020. https://www.gallup.com/cliftonstrengths/en/312830/create-culture-inspires-name-claim-aim-strengths.aspx.

Gallup. "How to Improve My Career: 02 What Career is Right for Me?" *CliftonStrengths*. Accessed January 5, 2022. https://www.gallup.com/cliftonstrengths/en/299855/how-to-improve-my-career.aspx#ite-304610.

Morgan Roberts, Laura, Gretchen Spreitzer, Jane E. Dutton, Robert E. Quinn, Emily D. Heaphy, and Brianna Barker. "How to Play to Your Strengths." *Harvard Business Review*, January 2005. https://hbr.org/2005/01/how-to-play-to-your-strengths.

Winn, Marc. "What is your Ikigai?" May 14, 2014. https://theviewinside.me/what-is-your-ikigai/.

World Economic Forum. "The Future of Jobs Report 2020." October 2020. Accessed May 29, 2022. https://www3.weforum.org/docs/WEF_Future_of_Jobs_2020.pdf.

CHAPTER SEVEN

Harrin, E. "4 Types of Stakeholders in Project Management." *PM Tips* (blog). August 6, 2010 (revised August 7, 2020). Accessed March 26, 2022. https://pmtips.net/article/4-types-of-stakeholders-in-project-management.

Indeed. "A Comprehensive Guide to Stakeholders in the Workplace." March 1, 2021. Accessed April 10, 2022. https://www.indeed.com/career-advice/career-development/stakeholders-in-the-workplace.

Marcuslemonis.com. Marcus' 3P's of Business. Accessed June 9, 2022.
https://www.marcuslemonis.com/business/3ps-of-business

The MindTools Content Team. "Stakeholder Analysis: Winning Support for Your Projects." MindTools. Accessed March 26, 2022.
https://www.mindtools.com/pages/article/newPPM_07.htm.

Project Management Institute. *Project Management Body of Knowledge (PMBOK Guide)*. 6th ed. Newton Square, PA: Project Management Institute, 2017. Referenced by Usmani, Fahad "What is the PMBOK Guide?" *PM Study Circle* (blog). September 11, 2021. Accessed April 10, 2022.
https://pmstudycircle.com/what-is-the-pmbok-guide/.

Sobel, Andrew, and Jerold Panas. *Power Questions: Build Relationships, Win New Business, and Influence Others*. New Jersey. John Wiley & Sons, Inc, 2012.

"What is a project stakeholder?" *Teamwork* (blog). Accessed March 26, 2022.
https://www.teamwork.com/project-management-guide/project-stakeholders/.

CHAPTER EIGHT

Busch, May. "3 questions to ask yourself before taking on a stretch assignment." *May Busch Creating Leaders* (blog). Accessed April 10, 2022.
https://maybusch.com/3-questions-ask-yourself-before-taking-on-stretch-assignment/.

PricewaterhouseCoopers (PWC). "Workforce of the future: The competing forces shaping 2030." Accessed October 2, 2021.
https://www.pwc.com/gx/en/services/people-organisation/workforce-of-the-future/workforce-of-the-future-the-competing-forces-shaping-2030-pwc.pdf.

Sobel, Andrew, and Jerold Panas. *Power Questions: Build Relationships, Win New Business, and Influence Others*. New Jersey. John Wiley & Sons, Inc., 2012.

CHAPTER NINE

Hasbe, Sudhir. "Half Of All Meetings Are a Waste Of Time—Here's How To Improve Them." *Forbes*. November 25, 2019. Accessed April 22, 2022.
https://www.forbes.com/sites/googlecloud/2022/03/04/90-of-companies-have-a-multicloud-destiny-can-conventional-analytics-keep-up/?sh=42d9a34f5d89.

Knaus, Bill. "It's Not What You Say—It's How You Say It!" *Psychology Today* (blog). November 19, 2013. Accessed May 13, 2022.
https://www.psychologytoday.com/gb/blog/science-and-sensibility/201311/it-s-not-what-you-say-it-s-how-you-say-it.

"Kweku Adoboli." *CFA Society.* Accessed May 13, 2022.
https://www.cfasociety.org/southafrica/Lists/Events%20Calendar/Attachments/290/Kweku%20Adoboli%20Bio.pdf.

MindTools. "Mehrabian's Communication Model: Learning to Communicate Clearly." Accessed May 13, 2022.
https://www.mindtools.com/pages/article/newCS_83.htm.

Perlow, Leslie. A., Constance N. Hadley, and Eunice Eun. "Stop the Meeting Madness." *Harvard Business Review*. Accessed April 21, 2022. https://hbr.org/2017/07/stop-the-meeting-madness.

Tschabitscher, Heinz. "19 Fascinating Email Facts." *Lifewire* (blog). March 15, 2020. Accessed April 21, 2022. https://www.lifewire.com/how-many-emails-are-sent-every-day-1171210.

CHAPTER TEN
Black Angel Group. Portfolio. 2021. Accessed June 12, 2022. https://blackangelgroup.com.

Bulao, Jacquelyn. "20 Eye-Opening Networking Statistics for 2022." *Techjury* (blog). May 02, 2022. Accessed May 13, 2022. https://techjury.net/blog/networking-statistics/#gref.

Busch, May. "Who you need in your network." *May Busch Creating Leaders* (blog). Accessed April 10, 2022. https://maybusch.com/wp-content/uploads/2017/05/Building_Your_Winning_Network_Workshop_Part_2_Who_You_Need_in_Your_Network.pdf

Fischer, Sara. "Exclusive: LinkedIn aims to close 'network gap.'" *Axios*. September 26, 2019. Accessed April 10, 2022. https://www.axios.com/2019/09/26/linkedin-inequality-network-gap-job-opportunities.

Freeland Fisher, Julia. "How to get a job often comes down to one elite personal asset, and many people still don't realize it." CNBC. December 27, 2019. Accessed April 10, 2022. https://www.cnbc.com/2019/12/27/how-to-get-a-job-often-comes-down-to-one-elite-personal-asset.html.

Ibarra, Herminia. "Building Effective Networks." March 24, 2016. Video, 15:06. https://www.youtube.com/watch?v=k115ePA_9SU.

Jennae, Michele. *The Connect Worker: A business parable that elevates networking to a whole new dimension.* Self-published, Amazon Digital Services, 2013. Kindle

LinkedIn. "Eighty percent of professionals consider networking important to career success." June 22, 2017. Accessed April 10, 2022. https://news.linkedin.com/2017/6/eighty-percent-of-professionals-consider-networking-important-to-career-success.

LinkedIn. "What is LinkedIn and How Can I Use It?" Accessed June 10, 2022. https://www.linkedin.com/help/linkedin/answer/a548441/what-is-linkedin-and-how-can-i-use-it-?lang=en.

LinkedIn. "Your Network and Degrees of Connection." Accessed June 10, 2022. https://www.linkedin.com/help/linkedin/answer/a545636/your-network-and-degrees-of-connection?lang=en.

Loizos, Connie. "The rise of the Black Angel Group inside of Alphabet." Tech Crunch. February 10, 2022.
https://techcrunch.com/2022/02/09/the-rise-of-the-black-angel-group-inside-of-alphabet/.

Spellman College. Courageous Conversations - Rosalind Brewer, C'84. February 11, 2021. Video, 59:13.
https://youtu.be/g8eoOpuv-cI.

CHAPTER ELEVEN

Anderson, Cameron, and Sebastien Brion. "Overconfidence and the Attainment of Status in Groups." *UC Berkeley: Institute for Research on Labor and Employment.* April 14, 2010.
https://escholarship.org/uc/item/5zz0q2r0.

Blackwell, Trish. "How to exude confidence." April 14, 2020. In *The Confidence Podcast.* Produced by Trish Blackwell. Podcast, MP3 audio, 35:50.
https://www.trishblackwell.com/386-2/.

Burnford, Joy. "Getting to Equal: Career Confidence And The Path To Leadership." *My Confidence Matters.* Press release, November 13, 2019.
https://static1.squarespace.com/static/5a56011f268b9649237ca29f/t/5dcbcf927ea48572f9f70894/1573638041162/Getting+to+Equal+Press+Release+13-11-2019.pdf.

Kay, Kathy, and Claire Shipman. *The Confidence Code: The science and art of self-assurance - what women should know.* New York. Harper Business, 2014.

Kay, Kathy, and Claire Shipman. "Why Some People Are Genetically Wired To Be More Confident." April 12, 2014.
https://www.businessinsider.com/some-people-are-genetically-wired-to-be-confident-2014-4?r=US&IR=T.

CHAPTER TWELVE

Beveridge, Harriet, and Ben Hunt-Davis. *Will it Make the Boat Go Faster?: Olympic-winning Strategies for Everyday Success.* Leicester UK: Matador (part of Troubador Publishing LTD), 2011.

Howarth, Alice. "Michelle Obama opens up about her struggles with self-doubt." *Harper's Bazaar,* February 28, 2021.
https://www.harpersbazaar.com/uk/celebrities/news/a35666346/michelle-obama-reveals-her-struggles-with-self-doubt/.

Kay, Kathy, and Claire Shipman. *The Confidence Code: The science and art of self-assurance - what women should know.* New York. Harper Business, 2014.

Kramer Bussel, Rachel. "Michelle Obama Memoir Becoming Hits 3 Million Sales Mark; New Book Tour Dates Announced." *Forbes,* December 13, 2018.
https://www.forbes.com/sites/rachelkramerbussel/2018/12/13/michelle-obama-memoir-becoming-hits-3-million-sales-mark-new-book-tour-dates-announced/?sh=3a16e07b62a4.

Leaf, Caroline. *Switch On Your Brain: The Key to Peak Happiness, Thinking, and Health.* Michigan: Baker Books, 2013

The New York Times. "Readers Have Been Eagerly Waiting for Barack Obama's New Memoir. Struggling Booksellers Have, Too." Dec 8, 2020. Accessed June 13, 2022. https://www.nytimes.com/2020/11/15/books/barack-obama-promised-land-memoir-publishing-bookstores.html.

The Times. "Michelle Obama on Becoming: 'This book affirmed the value of stepping into our fears.'" February 28, 2021. https://www.thetimes.co.uk/article/michelle-obama-on-becoming-this-book-affirmed-the-value-of-stepping-into-our-fears-nkzlkd72z.

Voss, Patrice, Maryse E. Thomas, J. Miguel Cisneros-Franco, and Étienne de Villers-Sidani. "Dynamic Brains and the Changing Rules of Neuroplasticity: Implications for Learning and Recovery." October 4, 2017. https://doi.org/10.3389/fpsyg.2017.01657.

CHAPTER THIRTEEN

Buddy, T. "An overview of substance use." March 19, 2020. https://www.verywellmind.com/substance-use-4014640#toc-illegal-drug-use.

Centers for Disease Control and Prevention. "Physical Activity." Accessed June 18, 2022. https://www.cdc.gov/physicalactivity/basics/pa-health/index.htm

Fraga, Juli. "A Guide to Burnout." *Healthline* (blog). Medically Reviewed by Timothy J. Legg. May 18, 2019. Accessed June 12, 2022. https://www.healthline.com/health/tips-for-identifying-and-preventing-burnout.

Frieden, Tom. CDC Online Newsroom—Press Briefing Transcript. "CDC Vital Signs: Walking Among Adults—United States, 2005 and 2010 Telebriefing." August 7, 2012. http://www.cdc.gov/media/releases/2012/t0807_walking.html. Quoted in Johns Hopkins Bloomberg School of Public Health in collaboration with the Transamerica Center for Health Studies. "From Evidence to Practice: Workplace Wellness that Works." 2015. Accessed June 22, 2022. https://transamericainstitute.org/docs/default-source/jhu/from-evidence-to-practice---workplace-wellness-that-works.pdf?sfvrsn=dcbd5e9b_2.

Gallup (2019). "Gallup's perspective on Employee Burnout: Causes and Cures." Accessed February 8, 2022. https://www.gallup.com/workplace/282659/employee-burnout-perspective-paper.aspx.

Harvard Health. "The importance of hydration." Accessed February 1, 2022. https://www.hsph.harvard.edu/news/hsph-in-the-news/the-importance-of-hydration/.

Headspace. "Sleep 101." Accessed February 2, 2022. https://www.headspace.com/sleep/sleep-101.

Hrechka, Nicole, and Callie Woodley. "Fueling Productivity Through Nutrition." Wellness Works Canada. February 25, 2021. https://www.resources.wellnessworkscanada.ca/post/fueling-productivity-through-nutrition.

Johns Hopkins x Bloomberg School of Public Health in collaboration with the Transamerica Center for Health Studies. "From Evidence to Practice: Workplace Wellness that Works." 2015. Accessed June 22, 2022. https://transamericainstitute.org/docs/default-source/jhu/from-evidence-to-practice---workplace-wellness-that-works.pdf?sfvrsn=dcbd5e9b_2.

Marie, Jenny. "Millennials and Mental Health." National Alliance on Mental Illness (NAMI). Feb 27, 2019. https://www.nami.org/Blogs/NAMI-Blog/February-2019/Millennials-and-Mental-Health.

Marks, Hedy. "Stress Symptoms." *WebMD*. Medically Reviewed by Smitha Bhandari on August 19, 2021. Accessed February 8, 2022. https://www.webmd.com/balance/stress-management/stress-symptoms-effects_of-stress-on-the-body

Matakas, Chris. *My Mastery: Continued Education Through Jiu-Jitsu. Self-published*, 2013.

OECD (2011). "Chapter 6: Summary and conclusion." *Myths and Realities about Mental Health and Work*. OECD Publishing. Paris. Accessed February 8, 2022. https://www.oecd.org/els/emp/49227343.pdf.

OECD (2014), *Mental Health and Work: United Kingdom*, Mental Health and Work. OECD Publishing. Paris. Accessed October 2, 2021. https://doi.org/10.1787/9789264204997-en.

OECD (2013), *OECD Employment Outlook 2013*, OECD Publishing. Paris. Accessed October 2, 2021. https://doi.org/10.1787/empl_outlook-2013-en.

Pryce-Jones, Jessica. *Happiness At Work: Maximizing Your Psychological Capital for Success*. New Jersey. John Wiley & Sons, Inc., 2010.

Ratna, Abhishek. *No Parking. No Halt. Success Non-Stop!* New Delhi, India. Supernova, 2015.

Stansfeld, Stephen, Charlotte Clark, Paul Bebbington, Michael King, Rachel Jenkins, and Stephen Hinchliffe. "Common mental disorders." *In McManus S, Bebbington P, Jenkins R, Brugha T. (eds.) (2016) Mental health and wellbeing in England: Adult Psychiatric Morbidity Survey 2014*. Leeds: NHS Digital. Accessed June 14, 2022. https://assets.publishing.service.gov.uk/government/uploads/system/uploads/attachment_data/file/556596/apms-2014-full-rpt.pdf.

Thompson, Karl. "What Percentage of Your Life Will You Spend at Work?" ReviseSociology. August 16, 2016. https://revisesociology.com/2016/08/16/percentage-life-work/

Warburton, Darren E.R., Crystal Whitney Nicol, and Shannon S.D. Brendin. "Health benefits of physical activity: the evidence." *Canadian Medical Association Journal* 174, no. 6 (March 2006): 801–809. https://doi.org/10.1503/cmaj.051351.

World Health Organization. "Burn-out an 'occupational phenomenon': International Classification of Diseases." May 28, 2019. https://www.who.int/news/item/28-05-2019-burn-out-an-occupational-phenomenon-international-classification-of-diseases.

World Health Organization. "Constitution." *Governance*. June 19, 1946. https://www.who.int/about/governance/constitution.

World Health Organization. "Investing in Mental Health." 2003. Accessed February 8, 2022. https://apps.who.int/iris/bitstream/handle/10665/42823/9241562579.pdf?sequence=1&isAllowed=y.

World Health Organization. "Mental Disorders." November 28, 2019. https://www.who.int/news-room/fact-sheets/detail/mental-disorders.

World Health Organization. "World Mental Health Day: An opportunity to kick-start a massive scale-up in investment in mental health." August 27, 2020. https://www.who.int/news/item/27-08-2020-world-mental-health-day-an-opportunity-to-kick-start-a-massive-scale-up-in-investment-in-mental-health.

CHAPTER FOURTEEN

"Advertising." Entrepreneur Europe. 2022. Accessed May 13, 2022. https://www.entrepreneur.com/encyclopedia/advertising.

Fielding-Singh, Priya, Devon Magliozzi and Swethaa Ballakrishen. "Why Women Stay Out of the Spotlight at Work." *Harvard Business Review*. August 28, 2018. https://hbr.org/2018/08/why-women-stay-out-of-the-spotlight-at-work.

Moorman, Christine. "Top Ten Results from the February 2020 CMO Survey." *The CMO Survey* (blog). February 26, 2020. https://cmosurvey.org/top-ten-results-from-the-february-2020-cmo-survey/.

Printed in Great Britain
by Amazon

14829812R00200